Haunted Battlefields
of the South

Haunted Battlefields
of the South
Civil War Ghost Stories

Bryan S. Bush and Thomas Freese

4880 Lower Valley Road Atglen, Pennsylvania 19310

Other Schiffer Books on Related Subjects
Haunted Battlefields: Virginia's Civil War Ghosts.
Beth Brown. ISBN: 9780764330575. $14.99
Kentucky Spirits Undistilled.
Lisa Westmoreland-Doherty. ISBN: 9780764331428. $14.99

Schiffer Books are available at special discounts for bulk purchases for
sales promotions or premiums. Special editions, including personalized
covers, corporate imprints, and excerpts can be created in large quantities
for special needs. For more information contact the publisher:

Published by Schiffer Publishing Ltd., 4880 Lower Valley Road, Atglen, PA 19310
Phone: (610) 593-1777; Fax: (610) 593-2002, E-mail: Info@schifferbooks.com

For the largest selection of fine reference books on this and related
subjects, please visit our web site at **www.schifferbooks.com**
We are always looking for people to write books on new and related subjects.
If you have an idea for a book please contact us at the above address.

This book may be purchased from the publisher.
Include $5.00 for shipping.
Please try your bookstore first.
You may write for a free catalog.
In Europe, Schiffer books are distributed by
Bushwood Books
6 Marksbury Ave.
Kew Gardens
Surrey TW9 4JF England
Phone: 44 (0) 20 8392 8585; Fax: 44 (0) 20 8392 9876
E-mail: info@bushwoodbooks.co.uk
Website: www.bushwoodbooks.co.uk

Designed by "Sue"
Type set in Americana XBd/Aldine 721 BT

ISBN: 978-0-7643-3385-9
Printed in the United States of America

Contents

Acknowledgments

Special Thanks to the following: Elvin Smith, Jr., Wayne Peters, Gaye Clark, Sheri Britton, Patricia and John Aaron, Matt Aaron, Phil Seyfrit, and to the many Civil War re-enactors who provided their stories. Special thanks must also go to Roberta Simpson Brown for editing assistance and Jane Freese who did the digital art layout for the cover.

Introduction

Apparently Civil War soldiers still inhabit the battlefields of our Southern States. Is there an objective reality, which we can label with the term *ghost* and are the many odd, post-battle events evidence of activity of those same souls who perished in battle? Frequent and persistent accounts are told by the visitors to battle locations and those who live close to the long ago but poignant war sites. For years, both authors have heard first-hand accounts of dramatic and sensorial encounters with dead soldiers from this great and tragic war. Although not our last war and neither our nation's first violent conflict, the Civil War nevertheless brought widespread grief, injury, death, and agonizing injuries to both the bodies and psyches of the soldiers and civilians in our States.

Veteran re-enactor and historian Bryan Bush traveled to numerous Civil War Battlefields and researched both the tactical history and on-the-ground life of soldiers on both sides of the War. He interviewed re-enactors and photographed the places and people who immersed themselves in recreating the soldiers' camp, social, travel, and martial activities. Mr. Bush approached co-author Thomas L. Freese, author of numerous books on ghost stories, to work together to bring these fascinating tales to the greater public. Mr. Freese audio recorded stories from Civil War re-enactors and visitors to some of the battlefields of the War Between the States.

With the rise of ghost hunter societies and parapsychology, the study of ghosts has taken on a whole new realm of technical research and rational inquiry. Many believe that ghosts are souls who do not know they are dead and continue to lead their lives in the places they were happy or comfortable. Some believe certain areas attract ghosts because the place traps energy of those who lived there for years.

Still others feel that in the cruel battlefields where young men's lives were struck down in horrific moments that the energetic imprint of that moment is trapped forever. In this manner, the tragic event continually repeats like a broken record. Soldiers re-enact their deaths over and over again. At the battlefields of Perryville, Shiloh, and Franklin and at countless other named and unnamed places, unfortunate young soldiers made the ultimate sacrifice, yet they continue to relive their moments of agony and death. From some reports it also seems that some remnant of psychic energy is trapped in certain artifacts, which the men carried into battle. Disturbing energies and discarnate voices attach to such things as swords, rocking chairs, and military surgeon's boxes.

The soldiers ran through a variety of emotions while enlisting, training, traveling, and fighting. They may have felt elation, excitement, brotherly love, boredom, loneliness, frustration, anger, righteous idealism, bitter disappointment, disgust, self-loathing, guilt, and dozens of other feelings. Some sightings of Civil War ghosts seem not to be of the dead killed in battle but rather simply those who served or, then again, at prewar camps where they were indeed carefree.

One can understand why there may be so many ghosts on our Civil War battlefields when the grim statistics of the war are taken into account. During the Civil War, one out of every 42.7 Union soldiers was killed in battle, one out of every 6.7 men was wounded and one out of 10.2 Union soldiers was captured and sent to prisoner of war camps. Of every seven Union soldiers captured, one died in prison. The Union army lost 110,000 soldiers killed in battle while the Confederates lost around 94,000 soldiers.[1] Although battlefield losses were staggering, disease was the main factor involved in soldiers' deaths. Of the 623,026 soldiers who died during the Civil War, an estimated 388,580, or sixty-two percent died of disease.[2] In all, 76,000 men from Kentucky served in the Union while 25,000 men from Kentucky fought for the Confederacy. At every Western Theater battle, Kentuckians fought Kentuckians. Ten thousand Kentuckians were killed in battle during the war and twenty thousand Kentuckians were victims of disease and exposure. Kentucky Historian Thomas Clark pointed out

Burying the dead at a hospital in Fredericksburg, Virginia. *Courtesy of the Library of Congress.*

the startling fact that approximately half the Kentuckians who reached manhood during the decade 1850-1860 were either killed or disabled by the war.[3]

One of the leading causes of death on the battlefield was the Minie ball. The then newly developed Minie ball, when shot from a rifle and then impacting human tissue, muscle or bone at high speed, caused massive destruction of the human body. The soft lead projectiles smashed bone and ligaments. Amputations were the only way a surgeon could save a life. Doctors very often received patients with multiple wounds. Patrick Cleburne, who was killed at the battle of Franklin, Tennessee, received forty-nine bullet wounds. When a surgeon arrived on the scene at the field hospital, he often used a door and two barrels for an amputation table. The following overview of the state-of-the-art of medical treatment post-battle involves graphic descriptions and might be skipped by those sensitive to discussions of blood and gore.[4]

The surgeon applied a tourniquet to the area to be amputated and the patient was given chloroform if it was available. The surgeon used his finger to probe for the bullet and if the bullet were deep he would use a longer metal probe. Once the bullet was found, the surgeon pried the bullet out with a bullet extractor. If damage to the area was too massive then the surgeon performed an amputation. However, most amputations were performed to

Union re-enactor soldiers at rest on the Perryville, Kentucky, Battlefield.

prevent septicemia and gangrene. The surgeon cut at an angle forming a point and the skin was pulled back to expose the bone. The surgeon then sawed off the limb.[5]

He then put a ligature on the arteries to prevent bleeding. The ligature was applied by looping thread around the ruptured artery leaving the end of the thread dangling from the wound or incision. Every day the surgeon would tug at the thread until the loop had rotted and the remaining strand came away in his hand. The only problem with this procedure was that if the artery wall had any infection or if the clot had not formed, then the tugging opened the artery and the patient bled to death. Unfortunately, this fatal outcome occurred in two out of three cases in which the artery was opened up.[6]

Surgeons had to act quickly to stave off infection and blood loss, so most amputations were done within twenty-four hours. In January of 1862, after the Battle of Mill Springs, Kentucky, Union Surgeon David Smith wrote about the conditions after the battle:

> ...the dreadful roads over which all of the wounded had been brought had induced profuse suppuration. All the food that could be procured was beef, pork, and hard bread. Shortly after my arrival I saw one man die from the irritation produced by fragments of the upper jaw, which although split in every direction by passage of a Minie ball, had been left without excision. The same state of things existed also in the case of a fractured lower jaw, and was followed by the same result. Two cases of gunshot wounds of knee joint, in which amputation had not been performed, also came to a rapidly fatal termination. In four cases of gunshot fracture of the humerus, reported to me as doing well, I found such complete comminution that in two cases I excised large portions of the shaft and in the remaining two, the head of the bone...[7]

Blood transfusions were unknown to most surgeons at that time. Thus, every drop of blood shed by the patient would put him one step closer to death. Abdomen and head wounds were fatal ninety percent of the time. And it is sad to say that if the small intestine was involved then death was inevitable. The mortality rate for chest wounds was sixty percent. Surgeons did not have the knowledge to repair such massive wounds to vital areas or to prevent internal bleeding.[8]

Since there was no concept of sterilization of instruments or the use of antiseptics to combat infection, soldiers very often came down with tetanus, blood poisoning, and gangrene. Surgeons very often went without washing their hands or instruments. Pyaemia, or blood poisoning, comprised forty-three percent of all deaths from primary amputations and was usually ninety-seven percent fatal once the patient acquired the disease. Infections were the chief cause of mortality following surgery and also for untreated wounds.

Surgeons thought that laudable pus was a good sign of healing and usually encouraged the formation of pus on the wound. Doctors often used water dressings, which usually encouraged gangrene and infections. S. H. Melcher, Assistant Surgeon in the 5th Missouri Volunteers, at Wilson Creek, reported in 1861:

> The wounded were sent to the rear in wagons as the fight progressed. The attendance they received was trifling, consisting of water dressings or adhesive plasters. The flies were exceedingly troublesome after the battle, maggots forming in the wounds in less than an hour after dressing them, and also upon any clothing or bedding soiled with blood or pus. The wounded left on the field in the enemy's hands were swarming with maggots when brought in. After several ineffectual attempts to extirpate these pests, I succeeded perfectly by sprinkling calomel freely over the wounded surface. When the sloughs separated, clean granulating surfaces were presented, and by using balsam of [copaiba] as a dressing, smearing the bandages with this oleoresin, I could keep the wounds free from maggots.

Unlike Surgeon Melcher, many doctors saw that maggots were actually beneficial, since maggots only destroy the dead flesh and will not touch the healthy flesh.

Surgeons did not have the knowledge of how to administer medication properly and they always ran the risk of under medicating or over medicating their patients. Surgeons were also not aware of the addictive effects of some medications, like opium and morphine. After surgery, many patients suffered withdrawal symptoms and after the war thousands were lifetime drug addicts. Alcoholism was also a major problem. Boredom or the proclivity for surgeons to use the numbing effects of alcohol upon their patients often led to soldiers suffering from Detoxing Tremors. Surgeons were not immune to the gore and boredom they faced every day and they themselves succumbed to the effects of drug addiction and alcoholism. The Civil War occurred during the age when there were no x-ray, antibiotics, vitamins, concentrates, plasma or vaccines to prevent typhoid and tetanus. We were a nation at war, and America was still a budding young country.

In addition to the dramatic effect on the soldiers, civilians were affected by the conflict. Here is but one example of one day in the life of a young woman who wrote:

> This is quite a cool and gloomy morning for the month of July. Everything seems enshrouded in gloom. It seems as if everything is clad in mourning. Almost every heart is made sad about the late battles. Thousands of hearts and homes have been made desolate by this terrible war. When will it cease? Will not some kind fairy step forward and whisper in our ears the welcome word? Will not the time soon come when all will be joy and happiness? Hardly a day passes but we hear of the death of some dear friend, some friend that has been sent to his long home by the hand of an enemy. Death, death the terrible messenger comes upon us slowly but surely and snatches the life of some dear friend. Such sad feelings I have never before experienced, as now pervades my being. It seems as if nothing but gloom surrounds me. Even the merry prattle of children cannot dispel it. But we will hope for the best, hope that all again will be bright and beautiful.[9]

In many places, the Civil War was fought in residents' towns, homes, and farm fields. After the battle, these same barns, homes, and churches served as makeshift hospitals. The Battle of Perryville occurred on most of Squire Henry P. Bottom's farmland. After the Battle of Perryville, the Goodnight House and the Russell House served as hospitals. Squire Bottom, with the help of his field hands, gathered up most of the Confederate dead on his land and placed them in piles. Bottom tried to record the names, insignia or identifying marks on the bodies to help identify them when relatives came looking for their fallen loved ones. Bottom dug a massive grave on top of the hill, near Parson's Battery, with two rows of pits, four pits on each side, for four hundred Confederate dead. Most of the Union dead were buried in graves along the Springfield Road on Peter's Hill but after the war, the bodies were disinterred and reburied at Camp Nelson cemetery and at Lebanon, Kentucky.

Most of the fiercest fighting during the Battle of Richmond, Kentucky, took place at the Mount Zion church, the Rogersville/White Road, and the edge of Richmond, including the cemetery. In December of 1862, Confederate General John Hunt Morgan attacked Elizabethtown, Kentucky, and shelled the town. During the Battle of Corydon, Indiana, General Morgan sent cannon balls into Thomas McGrain's lawn. The civilian towns of Vicksburg (Mississippi), Atlanta (Georgia), Chattanooga, Franklin, Nashville, and Knoxville (Tennessee) became battlefields. The individual non-combatants living in these cities faced hunger, poverty, and displacement from their homes. Since the men fought in the war, women and children were left to run the farms. They suffered from food shortages and the devaluation of the currency—which led to many families doing without the bare necessities of life. Union armies and Confederate guerillas burned or pillaged homes, livestock, and crops in the Southern farm fields,

Confederate artillery preparing their guns for battle at the re-enactment of Franklin and Nashville, Tennessee.

Squire Bottoms Historical Marker located in front of the Bottoms House. After the Battle of Perryville, the Squire Bottoms House became the scene of carnage and death as surgeon J. J. Polk operated on wounded soldiers in the house. Bullet holes can still be seen today inside the house as a reminder of the horrific battle.

cities, and towns. With thousands of men killed during the war, women could no longer afford their homes or to take care of their children. During the Victorian age, women had few options for work to support their families. With their husbands killed during the war many women had no choice but to give their children to orphanages.

Many modern residents of these Southern states surely must co-habit old mansions and other homes with the spirits of the Civil War. Some homes were converted to host overnight visitors in the bed and breakfast business, where they find guests at breakfast, wide-eyed, telling of nightly spectral visions of a field hospital in operation in the bedroom. Soldiers still walk the streets asking for water. You don't have to be a re-enactor to encounter a Civil War ghost!

We cannot be prepared for the unexpected. We may not be able to produce the ghosts from the Civil War on demand or at our convenience. But we can enter into their time, study the troop movements, and imagine what their camps were like. Every battle is a book of stories unto itself but overall the pattern of these first-hand accounts is clear. The ghosts see us as real. They drift into the re-enactors camp at breakfast. They pick up an apple from a table by the re-enactor's tent. They grab visitors by the shoulders and entreat, "Never again let this happen!"

They ask for water and wander bloodied through our hallways. They ask us to see what happened, look at their wounds, and understand the great sacrifices they made. The Civil War spirits honor us by appearing in our midst to communicate the human need for understanding, acceptance, and the compelling grace of sharing some of their emotional pain. Here are the tales which will honor their memory and when told help them to rest after their second great job is done—teaching us to avoid the same perils of division and strife in our country.

Soldier in portrait. *Courtesy of the Library of Congress.*

The Battle of Perryville, Kentucky

Confederate Generals Braxton Bragg and Major General Edmund Kirby Smith met in Chattanooga, Tennessee, July 31, 1862, to plan their invasion of Kentucky. Both Generals were hoping to bring Kentucky into the fold of the Confederacy. Braxton Bragg had high hopes for Kentucky. Kentucky Confederate Cavalry General John Hunt Morgan promised that Braxton Bragg would be able to pick up 25,000 men if he entered this state. Bragg was also looking for badly needed supplies. Edmund Kirby Smith was the first to enter the state in August of 1862 and was very much supported by the locals as large crowds came out to greet him. At Lexington, Kentucky, Smith was greeted with Confederate flags waving as he entered the town.[1]

The greeting would not be the same for Bragg. Bragg entered the state in areas where Union support was very high. He was hoping to link up with Smith and then both armies were to march on Louisville. They were trying to get to Louisville before Union General Don Carlos Buell's Army of the Ohio arrived from Knoxville, Tennessee. Bragg was never able to link up with Smith and ended up fighting a battle at Munfordville, Kentucky, in September. The battle delayed Bragg long enough to allow Don Carlos Buell to arrive in Louisville first. While in Louisville, Buell picked up recruits and brought his army to 58,000 men. Bragg had about 15,000 men and Smith had the main army of about 25,000. Buell then secured Louisville and was awaiting Bragg. Buell's job was on the line and he knew that he had to win a victory or else. Buell originally did not want the job of commanding the Army of the Ohio. But Union General Jefferson Davis killed the commanding officer before him, General William "Bull" Nelson, in the lobby of the Galt House in Louisville and Buell received the command by default. Buell was unaware of the true size of Bragg's army.[2]

During the summer of 1862, Kentucky was going through one of the state's worst droughts. Both armies were looking for water sources. Bragg heard that there was water at the Chaplin River, Doctor's Creek, Bull Run, and Wilson Creek in Perryville, Kentucky. Bragg arrived in Perryville first. William Hardee, along with Simon Buckner's Division, came in from the west along the Springfield Road on October 6th. They fell back from Bardstown, Kentucky, and hoped to settle in at Harrodsburg, Kentucky. Hardee stopped for water in Perryville, thinking that the Union army under Buell was to the north. He was confused when he saw heavy numbers of Union troops traveling along the Springfield Pike. Hardee asked for

Present photograph of Doctor's Creek, Perryville, where heavy fighting took place between Union and Confederate soldiers to try and gain control of one of the few remaining water sources.

support and was given two divisions from Leonidas Polk's corps, Patrick Cleburne's, and Anderson's. At 3:00 A.M. on October 7th, Anderson moved out with Patrick Cleburne following. Polk commented that the Union force approaching Hardee was not large. He was very wrong.[3]

The Yankee forces converging at Perryville were three corps strong, a total of sixty thousand men. General Buell's plan was to keep the Rebels guessing as to where his force was, thus hoping to prevent Bragg and Smith from linking up. The strategy worked. Buell moved northeast from Louisville with his main force while launching a feint toward Frankfort. McCook's corps were led by Joshua Sill and supported by Dumont. These twenty thousand men were to confuse Bragg as to the real direction of Buell's army. Bragg swallowed the bait and was sure that Buell was going to attack Harrodsburg.[4]

The Union army approached Perryville on three roads. On the Federal left, moving by the Mackville Road, were the three division corps of Major General Alexander McCook. On the Federal right flank, advancing on Perryville via the Lebanon Road, were the corps of Major General Thomas Crittenden, which also comprised three divisions. Occupying the center were the corps of Major General Charles Gilbert, moving towards Perryville on the Springfield Road. Gilbert arrived before McCook and Crittenden. This situation saw the Federals having to fight the Rebels to get the water since the Rebels already had the water sources secured.

Hardee deployed his forces and after positioning two of Buckner's three brigades between the Harrodsburg Pike and the Chaplin River, sent St. John Liddell to occupy Peter's Hill where the Turpin house was located.[5]

On October 7, 1862, General Buell was less than five miles from Perryville. McCook was eight miles outside of Perryville and Crittenden was to the south much farther away looking for water. Gilbert was moving forward on the Springfield Road, which was heavily patrolled by Confederate Joseph Wheeler's cavalry. Six miles outside the city, Robert Mitchell's division was halted. Union Brigadier General Phil Sheridan was brought up and formed on the front and right of Mitchell. At midnight, Lt. Col. Carroll sent companies A and E in advance of the skirmishers. They soon found Rebels across Peter's Hill and fell back when fighting broke out.[6]

At two o'clock, Sheridan sent the brigade of Col. Daniel McCook and Barnett's battery to occupy the heights in front of Doctor's Creek. McCook moved forward and chased the Confederates from Doctor's Creek and seized the heights beyond. Before sunrise, McCook reported to Sheridan that he held the high ground.

St. John Liddell ordered a counter attack with Sweet's Mississippi Battery, concentrating their fire on the woods of Peter's Hill. Captain Charles Barnett's Battery returned fire as Liddell's troops moved forward. McCook then ordered his men to open fire and received a galling fire in return. Sheridan and McCook watched as Gilbert ordered his men not to bring on an engagement.

Sheridan wanted the water at Doctor's Creek and ordered Col. Bernard Talbott's brigade to attack Liddell. Two Illinois regiments and a Missouri regiment attacked and drove Liddell back. Sheridan deployed his line way beyond the Federal main line and his flanks were dangerously exposed. Sheridan's victory misled Buell into thinking the enemy was in complete disarray. Buell put off the battle until the next day. The Federal command was relaxed when Bragg launched his major attack against McCook's corps.[7]

Buell thought that the main Rebel force was in front of him. He had received no reports from George Thomas regarding the size of the Confederate force and so grossly overestimated the number of Confederates facing him. Bragg assumed incorrectly that only a small Union force was in front of him. Buell knew his job was on the line and wanted to make sure that all his corps was ready before he launched his attack, which was a fatal mistake. Buell was at the Dorsey House, which was five miles outside of town, nursing an injured leg. He was thrown off his horse on October 7th. The only corps that was in position was McCook's. Buell had no idea where his second in command, George Thomas, was located. Thomas was actually moving with General Crittenden's corps. The terrain was also a problem for Buell because he never heard heavy rifle fire. Buell was not even aware that a battle was being fought on the eighth of October until it was too late.[8]

Union General James Jackson marched his division in behind Rousseau's division as Starkweather's unit came up from the rear. McCook halted his men west of the Benton Road and set his corps headquarters at the Russell House, located on the Mackville Road just east of its intersection with the Benton Road. General Lovell Rousseau was on the Benton (White) Road, on Gilbert's left flank. Jackson placed his command on Rousseau's left. Rousseau ordered William H. Lytle to advance and allow his men to fill their canteens. On the left of Jackson was General William Terrill whose brigade was closest to the Chaplin River.[9]

Meanwhile, General Wharton's Confederate cavalry was joined by the 8th Texas Cavalry Regiment, the 4th Tennessee, and the 1st Kentucky Cavalry. They passed Cheatham's lines to the far right, crossing the Chaplin River. They moved into attack formation behind the hills, free from Federal observation. The charging cavalry surprised the 33rd Ohio Infantry Regiment on the bluff above the river and the Yankee pickets fled. Rousseau then halted the Confederate pursuit. The Federals assumed that the enemy was giving ground and that there would be no further Rebel attacks. The 42nd Indiana was cooking and eating when the Rebel attack wave broke upon them.

At 2:00 P.M., Cheatham gave the order to advance and the first line moved across the river. Jackson's and Rousseau's divisions were shocked to see the gray clad lines almost on top of them.

Polk and Cheatham yelled out, "Give it to 'em boys."[10]

Daniel Donelson's brigade advanced, followed closely by Alexander Stewart's command. Donelson's men were not prepared for the scene unfolding in front of them. In order to reach the Federals, they had to cross a depression in the terrain, which paralleled the enemy line. The 80th Illinois, 123rd Illinois, and the 105th Ohio were still taking their positions to form the Federal left. The Confederate attack was striking straight toward the Federal line. Donelson's brigade was facing Rousseau's division. Rousseau's was made up of the 2nd and 33rd Ohio of Harris brigade and the 24th Illinois—sent from John Starkweather's brigade along with Jackson's units to their right front. Parson's Federal battery, located beyond the line where Terrill's infantry was forming, soon fired on the right flank of Donelson's brigade while the battery of Samuel Harris opened up on his left flank.

Donelson's brigade was shattered, losing a third of his original strength. Alexander Stewart's brigade rushed to Donelson's aid, along with the 5th Tennessee regiment.[11]

Cheatham assigned George Maney's brigade the task of silencing the Yankee guns. Maney moved to the right, ascending the bluff and was able to go into attack formation while concealed from the Yankees both by a wooded area and a slight depression of the ground. From the left to right were the regiments of the 9th Tennessee and 6th Tennessee and the 41st Georgia. In reserve were the 1st and the 27th Tennessee. Thomas Malone,

Captain Samuel Harris's 19th Indiana Battery supported by the 80th Indiana Infantry engaged in battle with the 15th and 16th Tennessee Infantry Regiments of Brigadier General Alexander Stewart's Brigade. The Widow Gibson Barn can be seen in the distance. *Courtesy of the Library of Congress.*

Adjutant to General Maney, was placing the two reserve units when he heard artillery and musketry fire break out near the head of the column. Malone immediately rode out to find Maney standing near a great white oak tree at the edge of the field. In the field, he saw the 41st Georgia and the 6th and 9th Tennessee regiments on the ground, engaged in a bitter fight with the enemy on the edge of the hill in their front. The Federals were supported by Parson's battery of eight Napoleon guns. Confederate Turner's four six-pound howitzers were firing grape shot back at Parson's guns.

Maney's brigade plunged forward until the troops were only three hundred yards apart. The Yankees said the Rebels came out of nowhere. Left of the Union position, General James Jackson was with Parson's Battery as he moved his cannon and blasted into Maney's gray ranks. The 123rd Illinois also opened fire on the approaching Confederates troops.

Maney's columns confronted a fence and their advance came to a halt. Capt. James Hall, Company C, 9th Tennessee, told the story, "This fence had to be let down in some places to enable our officers to ride through. We lost a good many men here. After crossing the fence, our advance was up a steep incline until we reached a point where we could look down the muzzles of the enemy's guns, which were stationed just over the crest of the hill. Col. John Buford had been severely wounded at the fence and was compelled to retire from the field. The command transferred to Major G. W. Kelson, whose horse was shot in attempting to cross this same fence. Kelson thought it would be prudent for him to take the horse to the rear for treatment. This left us without Regimental officers, so that the left was the first to discover the position of the battery and a heavy line of infantry in its rear. At this point in our advance, we were brought under the fire of the battery not fifty feet in front of us and of the infantry line in its rear. Their fire was terrific and we were losing men rapidly, so much so that it caused our line to falter its advance."[12]

Maney realized if he stayed at the fence, his troops would be massacred, so he urged his men onward. Thomas Malone, adjutant to General Maney, said: "Every man was instantly on his feet, and I don't suppose that twelve hundred men ever gave such a yell before. With bayonets at charge they ran as fast as they could run right through the guns and over the enemy's line. We did not fire a shot from the time the charge began until the enemies' whole line of battle was in flight, and then, shooting deliberately, the butchery was something awful...I could walk upon dead bodies from where the enemy's line was established until it reached the woods, some three hundred yards away."

As the Confederates came screaming up the hill, Union General James Jackson remarked, "Well, I'll be damned, if this is not getting rather particular."

Right after he said these words, he was struck down and killed instantly. Colonel Field, commanding Company H, 1st Tennessee, was killed during the advance, all the while shooting his Spencer rifle. The 123rd Illinois fell back in panic. General Terrill ordered the regiment of seven hundred men forward when Maney's Rebels began their advance. Once Maney's men got past the fence, they raked the 123rd Illinois and the Yankees fled in fear.

Maney's fierce attack overran the Yankee position on their extreme left. Parson's battery lost half of its officers and men and most of its horses. Parson stood and drew his sword as if at parade rest, expecting to be killed. Parson's men finally pulled him away before he was captured. The Rebels next moved up Slocomb's battery alongside Parson's Battery. The hold on McCook's line collapsed. The Union troops stopped the Confederate onslaught at the Benton Road.

On Cheatham's left, Simon Buckner was driving Yankees before him. Buckner's men were opposed by Leonard Harris and William Lytle of Rousseau's division. Brig. General Thomas Jones made first contact with the Yankees and along with three Mississippi regiments, pounded them down a steep hill just north of Mackville Road and across the dry bed of Doctor's Creek. There the Union troops hit them with a volley of musket and artillery fire. The Mississippi troops returned fire. The 10th Wisconsin, which was on the left and the 42nd Indiana on the right, along with Peter Simonson's Indiana Battery, raked the Mississippians with gunfire. The Confederate advance was brought to a halt and the Mississippians retreated.

On Jones' left, Major General Simon Buckner's Rebel command was about to go in against Brigadier General Rousseau. Brigadier General

Bushrod Johnson, with his six regiments, was to spearhead the assault, while Brig. Gen. Daniel Adams, of Brigadier General J. Patton's Anderson's division, positioned himself on Johnson's left. His brigade was comprised of the 7th, 23rd, 25th, 37th, and 44th Tennessee and the 5th Confederate.

Johnson's brigade approached Doctor's Creek at the Mackville Road near Squire Bottom's House. Confusion prevailed when an oblique wheel to the left was attempted. Adams brigade marched to join Johnson's left flank. Johnson's Tennesseans lurched forward in a disjointed fashion. The most intense fighting broke out. The Confederate advance drove back the Federal skirmishers and quickly came to a halt. Several stone fences were south of the Mackville Road and both sides took advantage of them. Confederates began firing from the stone walls on the west bank of Doctor's Creek while Federals of the 3rd Ohio and 15th Kentucky crouched behind fences on the hillside west of the Bottom's House. Slocomb's battery blasted the Yankee troops. Col. John Beatty, of the 3rd Ohio, wrote, "For a time I do not know how long thereafter, it seemed as if all hell had broken loose; the air was filled with shot and hissing balls; shells were exploding continuously, and

Squire Bottoms House, Perryville, Kentucky: Owned by Squire H. P. Bottom, the house became a key position in the Battle of Perryville, on October 8, 1862. At the beginning of the battle, Union troops held the house. After a massed attack, Confederates took and held the house. After the battle, Bottoms identified and buried the CSA dead. The house also became the scene of carnage as Surgeon J. J. Polk performed amputations on the property.

the noise of the guns was deafening." There were two hundred dead from the five hundred-man Ohio regiment alone. General Rousseau said "Shiloh was nothing" compared to Perryville.

Daniel Adams' brigade was now on the flank held by the 3rd Ohio and the 15th Kentucky, who were being tormented by Slocomb's battery. Bushrod Johnson continued pressure on the front of the Federal line. Color bearer after color bearer went down. The 15th Kentucky lost nine and the 3rd Ohio lost all six color-bearers.

On Johnson's right, Brigadier General John Calvin Brown from Anderson's division, moved up to where Brigadier General Thomas Jones had been repulsed, applying pressure on the left flank. Brig. Gen. Patrick Cleburne was moving in front of Johnson and Brown. At double quick, Cleburne's men crossed the creek. While crossing the creek, Cleburne was shot in the ankle and his horse "Dixie" was killed but he continued to advance his men. A barn that was on fire forced the Yankees of the 3rd Ohio and the 15th Kentucky back up the hill and soon the entire Federal line followed them up the hill in full retreat. But the advance faltered when the Confederates were fired upon by their own artillery. Cleburne renewed the attack once the artillery was stopped.

The Confederates on the Benton Road continued their advance through a cornfield firing into the rear of the retreating Yankees. Gilbert's men saw from Peter's Hill the collapse of McCook's corps and Sheridan tried to help McCook by firing his artillery at the Confederate forces in the valley below him.

Buell ordered Gilbert to send a message to order Sheridan to stop firing his cannon and wasting ammunition. Sheridan and Gilbert were not engaged for the entire battle because Gilbert remained at Army Headquarters to eat with Buell. Sheridan quieted his artillery but he did not notify his corps commanders or the army commander that a battle was being fought off to his left.

The Rebels were placing two batteries on Sheridan's flank and massing troops behind them. Sheridan was on high ground and the Confederates tried four times to throw him off the hill but failed each time.

Starkweather held the ridge along the Benton Road, occupying the high ground and was responsible for saving the Union army from total defeat. As Terrill's brigade broke, they fled up the hill to Starkweather's position. Maney's brigade topped the ridge in front of Starkweather and began streaming down the western slope. Federal artillery on Starkweather's main line along Benton road opened on these Confederates. Stone's Battery A, Kentucky Light Artillery, was at the point where Benton Road turns west. Bush's Battery, the 4th Indiana Light Artillery, was on Stone's left. The 21st Wisconsin managed to hold off the Confederates approaching from the cornfield long enough to allow the regiments under Terrill to rally. The Union troops stood their ground, supported by Bush and Stone's Battery.

The 21st Wisconsin Regiment in the cornfield in front of Colonel John Starkweather's left and being advanced upon by Brigadier General George Maney's Brigade. *Courtesy of the Library of Congress.*

Confederate General A.P. Stewart marched to support Maney's men as they moved forward. The Union line laid down a heavy fire as Maney's troops struggled to the top of the ridge and grappled hand to hand with the Union troops. Maney's whole brigade became confused and disorientated. They retreated back down the slope where they rallied and once again charged back up the slope. The ground was slippery with blood around the cannons and on the hillside. The Rebels could not make it back up the bloody hill. Stewart and Maney called their men back. Maney's brigade lost half its men and Starkweather lost a third of his command. General Terrill was killed when an artillery shell exploded directly in front of him.

The battle was ending on the Yankee's extreme far left flank. Starkweather held firm but later that night he would pull back along the Benton Road to the west to lick his wounds.

At the Union center, General Rousseau learned that the brigades of Lytle and Harris had been driven to the Russell House where Lytle had been captured. The 15th Kentucky fell back from the Stone Wall and was now at the Russell House. Rousseau saw a heavy force on his right and ordered

Loomis Battery to open fire on them. They took a salvo from the Rebel guns in return. The Rebels made their attack at 2 o'clock and steadily advanced. General William Hardee ordered the Sam Wood Brigade, which consisted of the 16th and 33rd Alabama, the 3rd Confederate, the 45th Mississippi, 15th Mississippi Sharpshooters, and Semple's Alabama Battery, across Doctor's Creek to strengthen the attack. Wood's men formed on Cleburne's right flank as Cleburne's 2nd Tennessee, 13th Arkansas, and 15th Arkansas assaulted Webster's men, of the 98th Ohio, 42nd Indiana, and 80th Indiana at the Russell House. Cleburne's sharpshooters fired into Col. Harris's newly formed line, which was comprised of the 33rd Ohio and 10th Ohio, in front of the Russell House. Neither side gained an advantage.

Adam's brigade had advanced, driving the last of Lytle's brigade back across the Mackville Road, and was advancing along the roads towards the Russell House. As Adam's Brigade approached the 33rd Ohio and 10th Ohio, it opened fire. Rousseau ordered the 15th Kentucky and Loomis artillery to open fire. The 88th Indiana was ordered forward to support. Colonel George Humphrey, of the 88th Indiana, saw he was outnumbered and his men fell back up the hill towards the Russell house. It was ordered forward again to the top of the hill and along with the 15th Kentucky, opened a heavy fire upon Adam's brigade. Loomis's Battery opened up on Adams's Brigade but they kept on coming. McCook was now at the Russell House watching the battle. Harris now formed the 3rd Ohio, 38th Indiana, 10th Wisconsin, and 2nd Ohio into line across the Russell House to allow the 33rd Ohio and 10th Ohio to retire. The 10th Ohio and 33rd Ohio fell back to Harris's line. Adams's men followed, but discovered Harris's new line and halted. Adams ordered his men to fall back.

Cleburne ordered his brigade forward toward Harris's line across the Russell House. Cleburne came across the 88th Indiana, 15th Kentucky, 10th Wisconsin, 3rd Ohio, 2nd Ohio, and 38th Indiana. Cleburne halted.

Wood's brigade reached the hill west of Widow Bottom's house and saw Webster's Brigade about five hundred yards ahead. Wood ordered a charge. Webster ordered his artillery to withdraw. He only managed to pull out two pieces when Wood was right on him. The remaining four guns were manned by members of the 98th Ohio. Webster ordered the 80th Indiana to fall back to support the other two guns on a hill four hundred yards to the rear. Wood ordered a charge and the Union line gave way. The four artillery pieces were abandoned. The 42nd Indiana fell back to Harris's line. The 98th fell back to the line held by the 80th Indiana.

Buckner's artillery, which was composed of Slocumb, Darden, and Calvert, positioned above the Bottom House, fired at the Russell House. Simonson's Union battery fired back. Simonson's artillery ran out of ammunition and fell back. Buckner ordered the 25th and 44th Tennessee forward. They halted at a small ravine. Adams's Brigade moved past them on the right, falling back to the rear. An artillery duel broke out when the main Confederate effort shifted to Cleburne's right, where Union General Webster was killed. At 3:30 P.M. the Union troops received help from Gilbert in support of McCook. Col. Michael Gooding's brigade was sent to help. Gooding's brigade included the 59th Illinois, the 75th Illinois, and the 22nd Indiana. Gooding was opposed by Wood's brigade. Harris was ordered to fall back. As Harris fell back, Wood's brigade took position across the Russell House just vacated by Harris. Harris placed his regiments in line in front of the Benton Road.

Gooding formed his line in a wooded pasture to the right of the Benton Road. Gooding ordered his brigade forward. Wood opened fire on Gooding and Gooding fired back. Harris's line to Gooding's left gave way and then Gooding was all alone. Oscar Pinney advanced his artillery and opened fire from a position on a small hill across the Mackville Road, which tore great holes into the Confederate grey lines. The Confederates charged and charged but were repulsed. New grey clad soldiers filled the gaps. Twelve pieces of Confederate artillery at the Bottom House and Rebel infantry badly outnumbered Gooding's 1,550 men, so Liddell's Arkansas troops were thrown into the mix. Liddell moved to Gooding's exposed left flank. The 22nd Indiana, which was on Gooding's right, charged Wood's left, and Wood was severely wounded. Wood's brigade was ordered to retire. Wood's quartermaster, commissary, and assistant adjutant generals were all dead upon the battlefield.

Liddell now appeared before the 59th Illinois on Gooding's left. Gooding ordered the 22nd Indiana to the left. General Polk arrived at Liddell's position and saw what he believed to be Confederate soldiers firing into their own troops. Polk rode up to a Colonel of the regiment, which was firing. He asked him why he was shooting on his own men and told him to cease firing at once.

The Colonel said, "I don't think there can be any mistake about it, for I am damned certain that they are the enemy."

Polk said "Enemy! Why I have just left them myself. Cease firing, Sir. What is your name, Sir?"

"My name is Colonel Keith of the 22nd Indiana and, pray Sir, who are you?"

Polk quickly realized that he was in the middle of a Yankee regiment. Luckily Polk's dark frock coat helped him.

Polk shook his fist in front of the Yankee Colonel and said, "I'll soon show you who I am, Sir. Cease firing at once."

Polk quickly turned his horse around and headed back to his own lines expecting to hear a volley of fire into his back. Luckily Polk made it back to his own lines. Liddell poured heavy volleys into the 22nd Indiana. Col. Keith of the 22nd Indiana was shot down. Gooding's horse was shot and Gooding went tumbling down. Gooding's line collapsed and his men retreated northwest of the intersection of the Mackville and Benton Roads while Liddell stopped his advance at the intersection. As Gooding tried to escape, he was captured by the Eighth Arkansas. Col. Bennett took command.

The brigade fell back across the Mackville Road. Liddell advanced but was halted by Pinney's battery. Liddell ordered his men to cease firing, since the only means of seeing the enemy was by moonlight. Pinney's battery withdrew. Liddell went forward again. Captain Charles Swett's battery was sent forward and placed on a hill just vacated by Pinney. Pinney fell back to the Russell House hill. Liddell was ordered to halt. The Battle of Perryville was over.

After the battle, the fields were a scene of terror. Wounded, dying, and dead soldiers littered the battlefield. The first task was to care for the wounded soldiers. Liddell described, 'the fields and woods in front and around us on every side were strewn with the enemy's dead and wounded; their loss could hardly have been less than five hundred killed and wounded in the space of four to five acres.' The wounded collected by Liddell were sent to the Russell House and the house became filled with the bloody and mangled Confederate wounded. Unfortunately, Liddell did not provide for many of the wounded Union soldiers.

Sam Watkins, John Tucker, Scott Stephens, and A. S. Horsley of Company H, 1st Tennessee, helped bring the wounded off the field that night. Sam Watkins listed many of the slain: "Joe Thompson, Billy Bond, Byron Richardson, the two Allen boys—brothers killed side by side—and Col. Patterson, who was killed standing right by my side. He was first shot through the hand, and was wrapping his handkerchief around it, when another ball struck and killed him. I saw W. J. Whittorne, then a strapping boy of fifteen years of age, fall, shot through the neck and collarbone. He fell apparently dead, when I saw him all at once jump up, grab his gun, and commence loading and firing, and I heard him say 'D—n 'em, I'll fight 'em as long as I live'."[13]

"We brought off a man named of Hodge, with his under jaw shot off, and his tongue lolling out. We brought off Captain Lute B. Ivine. Lute was shot through the lungs and was vomiting blood all the while, and begging us to lay him down and let him die. But Lute is living. Also, Lieutenant Woldrige, with both eyes shot out. I found him rambling in a briar-patch. About fifty members of the Rock City Guards were killed and nearly one hundred wounded. Lieutenant Thomas Maney was badly wounded. I saw dead on the battlefield a Federal General by the name of Jackson. I cannot tell the one half, or even remember at this date, the scenes of blood and suffering that I witnessed on the battlefield of Perryville. Where are my old friends and comrades, whose names were so familiar at every roll call, and whose familiar 'Here' is no more? They lie yonder at Perryville, unburied, on the field of battle. They lie where they fell. More than three hundred and fifty members of my regiment, the First Tennessee, numbered among the killed and wounded—one hundred and eighty-five slain on the field of battle. They sleep the sleep of the brave."

Captain James Hall, 9th Tennessee, Co. C, was shot through the body while attacking the second Union position after the Yankees had fallen back from Parson's ridge. He fell in the grass of a bluegrass pasture. Some of the soldiers of his unit lifted him and set him underneath a tree for shade from the blazing sun. He had lost a tremendous amount of blood and did not remember being taken from the field. The next thing he remembered was being carried on an ambulance down a dry creek bed, and was carried for a long distance. The 9th Tennessee's hospital was located at the Goodnight farm. It was midnight when he reached the hospital. The surgeons pronounced Hall as mortally wounded and that he would not make it through the night. He was given a liberal dose of morphine to kill the pain by the doctor and placed under an apple tree. Two men were suffering from wounds similar to Hall's wounds and lay to either side of Hall. The two men constantly asked him questions about how he felt or whether he would last the night. Hall finally fell asleep and when he awoke, the two soldiers who were beside him had died during the night. After two days, he was placed under a temporary shelter constructed of boards and old planks found lying about the house. Hall was taken prisoner when the Yankees entered the camp hospital.

Confederate General Leonidas Polk returned that night to Perryville and while he stood in front of the Harmonia College on the hill behind the city, he began to hear music from the Union camp out on the Springfield Road. The air was filled with, "Home, Sweet, Home," which brought tears to every Confederate soldier. When the Yankees finished playing, the Confederate band, which was at the Harmonia College, repeated, "Home, Sweet, Home." Silence reigned over the battlefield.

After the battle, the town of Perryville became one huge hospital but unfortunately it had only one doctor, Dr. J. J. Polk. There was no hospital to handle the thousands of wounded and sick that were now everywhere. To make matters worse, General Buell ordered that all medical supplies be left behind in Louisville. Only one wagon was furnished for each brigade. According to G. G. Shumand, Surgeon for the United States, no hospital had been previously established anywhere.

> To add to this difficulty, no tents of any character were allowed the troops. As the march was long and fatiguing, while the nights were cool and disagreeable, the army suffered severely from diseases, and by the time it arrived at Perryville, the numbers of sick was unusually large...

Surgeon A.N. Read, U.S. Sanitary Commission, arrived on October 10, 1862, and found conditions had not improved in Perryville.

"We found the first hospital for the wounded at Maxville. This was a tavern, with sixteen rooms, containing 150 wounded and thirty sick, mostly from a Wisconsin regiment. Twenty five were on cots; some on straw; the others on the floor with blankets...From the place to Perryville, some ten miles away, nearly every house was a hospital. At one log cabin, we found twenty of the 10th Ohio, including the Major and two Captains. At another house were very poor, but doing all in their power for those in their charge. The mother of the family promised to continue to do so, but said, with tears in her eyes, she feared that she and her children must starve when the winter came."

Read went on to say that "at least 2,500 Union and Rebel soldiers were at that time lying in great suffering and destitution about Perryville and Harrodsburg..."

On October 11, twenty-one ambulances finally arrived in Perryville. By this time 1,800 soldiers were wounded in and around Perryville.

According to Read "they were all very dirty, few had straw or other bedding, some were without blankets, others had no shirts, and even now, five days after the battle, some were being brought in from the temporary places of shelter whose wounds had not been dressed. Every house was a hospital, are crowded, with little to eat..."

On October 12, Read, along with Dr. Goddard left for Danville. Conditions were not any better.

"Here we found the wants of the sick as urgent as those of the wounded at Perryville. The courthouse was literally packed; many had eaten nothing during the day, most of them nothing since morning...There was no water in the town-the wells were all dry."

Surgeon Read had a difficult time in procuring food for the sick soldiers as all the kettles were taken by the Rebels. There was no meat. Read managed to find two 32-gallon kettles and found a butcher who hauled water by barrel and slaughtered an animal. Read then found some salt and pepper and by 10 o'clock that night he managed to have soup for the soldiers.

On October 15, Read reached General Mitchell's Division. He found the soldiers suffering from exposure, since they had no tents and the food consisted of hard bread and bacon and no vegetables. Over ten percent of Mitchell's Division was sick. He also found that several of the regimental surgeons had no medications and were told not to take any.

Read commented that "The spirit of the army is not what it should be. Through the commanding General (by now it was General William Rosecrans) they are seriously demoralized."

Read returned to Danville and found "the number of sick considerably increased. As there were many who were without shelter."

Read found a carriage house owned by a Mr. J. W. Welch. Welch agreed to take his carriages out and straw was laid out for two hundred men. By the 18th, Read returned to Louisville.

On October 16, 1862, Surgeon G. G. Shumard said that the sick had increased so rapidly that it was necessary to establish large hospital depots for the sick and wounded.

"Perryville and Harrodsburg were already crowded with the wounded, (and) besides these, large numbers of sick, and wounded were scattered about the country in houses, barns, stables, sheds, or whatever they could obtain shelter sufficient to protect them from the weather...the Rebels during their retreat having left most of their sick and wounded behind, to nearly eight thousand...in two days the number of sick at this point (Danville) was increased to two thousand five hundred..."

The Methodist church in Perryville was also turned into a hospital. Members of the 3rd and 10th Ohio filled the church, using the pews as beds. Some Confederate wounded were also cared for in the church.

The battlefield was also a scene of mangled and mutilated bodies. Perry Hall of the 72nd Indiana marched with his unit a mile from Perryville and passed a hospital. He said there were "200 wounded. Many of their wounds never got dressed, and our men, who were on picket duty near them all night, described their cries and moans as piteous in the extreme."

John Berger, of the 29th Indiana, arrived two days after the battle and saw that there were "some 300 or 400 dead Sesh on the field unburied and I guess they lay there yet."

George Landrum, of the 2nd Ohio, said that Confederates were "lying two or three deep in some places" on the battlefield. He also saw Federal dead on the battlefield and commented that men had their heads shot off and were mangled in every possible manner.

Mead Holmes, Jr., of the 21st Wisconsin, marched with his unit through the battlefield of Perryville and "passed a cornfield of eighty acres almost covered with pens made of rails and covered with straw. These were filled with dead Rebels. It is said where so many died and there is no time to bury them they are piled up in this manner and burned. Unless something is done, the country is inhabitable. It is surprising how quick the dead become black, many lie with open eyes. One had died leaning against a tree and as we passed stared at us with that wild ghastly look that you could scarcely summon courage to meet."

Lewis Woody, 38th Indiana, Co. D, "the Rebels lay thick, they had stripped them also. Never do I want to see another such sight. It was awful to witness such a smell of human beings and the hogs eating the dead bodies."

A member of Harker's brigade wrote, "All round us was evidence of the death struggle the day before. Bodies of men and horses lay scattered about. In the fields and the roadside every house and barn was filled with the maimed and dying and the dead. Not far away lying upon the ground with no shelter from the sun by day and the dew by night, were some 300 Rebel wounded. They had as yet received no care from surgeons. Many of them were in the most horrible condition that the mind can conceive. Some were shot through the head, body or limbs. Others mangled by fragments of shell and are suffering the greatest torments."

ON THE MORNING AFTER THE BA
UNION FORCES OCCUPIED THE FI
THEY COLLECTED AND BURIED T
OWN DEAD BUT LEFT THE CONFED
WHERE THEY FELL   SQUIRE B
BOTTOM WHO OWNED THIS LANI
ING THE BATTLE COLLECTED NEAR
FALLEN CONFEDERAITS ON THIS
WITH THE HELP OF NEIGHBORS BU
THEM IN FOUR LARGE TRIANGULA
THIS ROCK WALL WAS BUILT ARI
THE CEMETERY SOMETIME LATER
UNION DEAD NOW REST IN CAMP
NATIONAL CEMETERY

Confederate Cemetery, located near Parson's Battery. After the battle of Perryville, Squire Bottom and his slave hands buried four hundred Confederate soldiers in a mass grave.

Dr. J. J. Polk, the town doctor in Perryville, rushed out to the Russell House to administer to the wounded that were scattered among not only the Russell House but also the Bottom's House.

Polk said that the Russell House was "dotted all over with musket and cannon balls. All around lay dead bodies of soldiers, Union and Reb."[14]

After the battle, Squire Bottom, with the help of field hands, set about gathering up bodies and placed them into piles. Most of the dead were around the Open Hill. Squire Bottom dug a huge trench around a hill where Parson's Battery was located. A stonewall now surrounds the present day site, which is located on the battlefield near the museum. There are four tombstones in the graveyard of those who were identified, the rest are lost to history.

As late as October 16, the Confederate dead still were not buried. A union soldier who was traveling through Perryville wrote "There are hundreds of men being eaten by the buzzards and hogs."[15]

The Union dead were buried in graves along the Springfield Road on Peter's Hill, but were later dug up and reburied at Camp Nelson, in Jessamine, Kentucky, and at Lebanon, Kentucky.

Close up view of the Confederate monument where four hundred Confederate soldiers are buried.

Union Monument dedicated to the Union soldiers of the Army of the Ohio who lost their lives during the Battle of Perryville.

It was a tactical victory for Bragg, but it was a strategic victory for the Union because Bragg would pull out from Perryville and move towards Harrodsburg. Once Bragg linked up with Edmund Kirby Smith, Bragg made for the Cumberland Gap and crossed back into Tennessee, never to return to Kentucky again. Casualties: 7,407 total (US 4,211: CS 3,196)

The Bottom's House Ghosts

In 1996, the Perryville Enhancement Project bought the Bottom's House and decided to renovate the house to its 1870 appearance. The only photograph they have of the house dates from 1870. The clapboard roof was put on and all the walls were stripped right down to the original beams. To the shock and surprise of the restoration crews, they discovered bullet holes littering the walls of the house. One bullet hole traveled from the front top bedroom of the house, through the mid-hall, and lodged in the back wall. Also, when the attic was opened, they found one of the original doors and it was blood stained. This door may have been the amputation table used by Dr. J. J. Polk.

During the grand celebration of the re-opening of the Bottom's House, several of the re-enactors portraying the 15th Kentucky and 3rd Ohio were allowed to stay in the house. One of the re-enactors said that when he entered the house, he became severely ill. He began to smell a sweet, putrid odor as if the smell of blood permeated the whole house. He got to the point of wanting to throw up and rushed outside.

Once he had gotten outside, he was just fine and the feeling passed. He did not re-enter the house. Could this re-enactor have re-lived the horrible experience of the house after the Battle of Perryville, when the house had become a place of butchery of men?

Another re-enactor stayed upstairs in the house during the night; he had heard nothing the whole night, but when he woke up the next morning he proceeded to walk down the stairs. All of a sudden, a force of some kind tried to push him down the stairs. Perhaps this was a Confederate soldier who had been brought to the house after the battle and was getting his revenge on his Union adversary.

The Ghosts of Parson's Battery

In 1995, a group of Confederate artillerists asked the park director if they could night fire on the battlefield. The park director agreed. Nothing is more exciting than watching a 12 pound Napoleon cannon firing at night. The raw force of artillery is brought out when cannon is fired at night. When the cannon is fired, an array of bright oranges, reds, and whites emerges from the tube. Sparks fly out as far as a hundred yards in front of the tube. Plus, when the dew of night starts to settle upon the battlefield, sound travels for miles and the smoke layers itself upon the battlefield, giving an eerie effect.

The artillery crew left their cannon on the battlefield near the hill of Parson's battery location, earlier in the afternoon where a re-enactment was held. The cannon were placed near where the battlefield cannons were actually located during the battle. The exact placing of the cannon was down the hill from where Union General Jackson was killed.

Five members of the artillery crew assembled about 9:30 P.M., along with other members of an infantry group. There were also children and wives who came out to watch the spectacular scene. It was a full moon that night and the battlefield was covered with the soft glow of the moon. The artillery crew always makes sure that the ground in front of the tube for about 400 yards is clear of people and that anyone in the immediate area is informed that a firing is about to take place.

One of the artillerists noticed that there were two Union soldiers on top of the bluff near where Union General James Jackson was killed. There was also a large white wall tent. They watched with their arms crossed. The artillerist of the cannon crew told his commanding officer. The commanding officer decided to send two of the daughters of the infantry men to run up the hill and inform Union observers that the artillery crew was about to do the first firing. The two girls quickly rushed up the hill and when they got midway up the hill, the two Union observers and the wall tent quickly vanished into thin air.

Years later, during the year 2000 re-enactment of the Battle of Perryville, several Union artillery pieces were placed exactly where Loomis battery had been placed 137 years ago. While they were waiting for the re-enactment to start, one of the re-enactors who had seen the Union ghosts at Parson' battery started to tell his story to his fellow re-enactors.

Present day scene of Parson's Battery, Perryville Battlefield. Two ghosts of Union soldiers have been seen at this location. Sounds of cannons being loaded have also been heard at Parson's battery.

One of the Union artillery re-enactors told him to stop in mid-sentence. Then with an excited look on his face, he quickly called over one of his buddies. As his friend arrived, the Union artillerist told him to continue the story about the 1995 re-enactment. After he had told his story, the Union artillerist said that they were walking the battlefield headed towards Parson's battery. As they approached the hill, they saw two Union soldiers watching them. They saw them in broad daylight and were even able to describe them. One of the Union soldiers had a beard and had his arm draped over his buddy's shoulder. As they got closer, the two Union soldiers disappeared.

Another ghost story that has been told to the author was about a re-enactment that occurred near the cannons on Parson's Hill. It was a moonlit night and several re-enactors decided to roam the battlefield at night. When they crossed down the hill in front of the guns, a unique sound that artillery makes was heard. The familiar "thud" was heard by two separate individuals. This sound is made when the rammer is being pulled from the cannon tube. The suction of the cannon tube upon cleaning on the end of the rammer provides the sound. When both re-enactors realized that a cannon tube was being cleaned, they whipped around and saw no one standing even near the tubes.

The Ghost in the Cornfield

Several re-enactors claimed to have seen a Confederate soldier wandering the cornfield, searching for his unit.

The Perryville Battlefield cornfield where Maney's Brigade encountered the 21st Wisconsin. A Confederate ghost has been seen in the cornfield.

The Ghost Fog

During the 125th and 130th Anniversary of the Battle of Perryville, there were many witnesses to the ghostly fog. At the present day site of the battlefield, there is a dry small creek bed along the bottom of the Open Hill. The fog appears, starting from the Benton-White Road, and advances slowly along the dry creek bed until it stops around the present location of the museum. Re-enactors claimed that they have heard the clacking and rattling of canteens, cups, and equipment. They also hear the thuds of footsteps advancing across the field.

The Confederate Soldier on Merchants Row

Another soldier ghost inhabits Merchants Row and is usually seen on the anniversary weekend in Perryville, which is usually held the first weekend in October. Perryville fills with hundreds if not thousands of people visiting the battlefield and also Merchants Row. Merchants Row was where many of the Union and Confederate wounded were taken to shelter in the local stores and houses.

Present day photograph of Merchants Row, Perryville, Kentucky. The ghost of a Confederate soldier has been seen in the cave under Merchant's Row and has also been seen in the street and some of the buildings. Fighting occurred in the streets between Confederate Colonel Samuel Powell's brigade and Union William Carlin's brigade.

The particular ghost that inhabits Merchants Row is a Confederate soldier looking for water. He comes up to a tourist and asks for a drink of water. The tourist will feel sorry for the thirst-starved soldier and enter the River Cafe on Merchants Row to get a glass of water. When the tourist returns with the glass of water for the soldier, he is nowhere to be found.

This same apparition has also been seen in the cave that runs under Merchants Row.

Not too long ago, one of the stores on Merchants Row became a bookstore. The local proprietor told the story of the ghost therein. As customers entered the store, a small bell rung as the door swung open. One night, as the storeowner slept, the door started to ring. She got up to see if anyone entered the store but the door was locked tight. When she returned to bed, the door rang again. She finally got frustrated with the prankster and told him to stop ringing the bell. Then it became quiet.

Later that season, a friend of the owner's visited the store. Late in the evening, the visitor looked out the large window facing the street and saw a bluish-green glow. Within that glow was a man of small stature wearing a Confederate uniform. She quickly turned away and walked to the living quarters. The next day her friend finally got enough courage to ask the storeowner if she had seen anything strange in the store.

The storeowner answered back, "Why, yes, late at night, the Confederate soldier will appear in the window."

Both agreed that the figure was always cast with a blue green glow.

The Confederate Soldier Who Inhabits Starkweather's Hill

This Confederate ghost was seen by three different witnesses at three different times but it was always the same ghost.

One Confederate re-enactor said that during one of the re-enactments a couple of years ago, he had to go "relieve himself." He decided to pick an area of small cedar trees that is in the middle of a field just behind Starkweather's Hill. While he was relieving himself, a Confederate soldier walked by him. This Confederate re-enactor was very much impressed with this soldier's look.

The Confederate soldier's dress was dirty and weathered. His hair was wet with sweat. What impressed him the most was the way he carried his rifle. It was campaign style, which has the tube of the rifle pointed downward. The reason for this is so that if it would happen to rain, the moisture would not fall into the barrel and rust it. Also, if the rifle was loaded and went off, it would not blow a hole in the soldier's head.

The Karrick Parks House, located on Merchant's Row, in Perryville, was used by Confederate officers and soldiers before the battle. After the battle, Union officers and surgeons used the house for six months. A ghostly apparition of a Confederate officer has been seen in the second story window.

Interpretative Center located on Merchants Row, Perryville, Kentucky.

The Confederate re-enactor looked at the Confederate soldier and nodded. The soldier said nothing and continued to walk on towards the small strip of trees that lies in back of Starkweather's Hill. The Confederate re-enactor turned quickly to see where the soldier was headed. The Confederate soldier vanished quickly without a trace.

Later that day, the Confederate re-enactor met a friend of his who was a Union re-enactor. The Confederate re-enactor started to tell the Union re-enactor his amazing story. The eyes of the Union soldier suddenly got wide and when asked why he had such an odd look on his face, the Union soldier said that he saw the same ghost.

The Union re-enactor was located at the front of the park and he saw the same Confederate soldier walking towards him from the Chaplin River, headed towards where the front entrance of the park is today. The Union soldier was also impressed with the Confederate soldier's appearance and said "Hi" to him. The soldier said nothing and continued to walk towards the Open Hill where Parson's battery is located. The Union re-enactor also watched the Confederate soldier disappear before his eyes.

The third witness to see this ghostly apparition was passing through the same line of trees that is in back of the Starkweather's position. He was also a Confederate re-enactor and said that the Confederate soldier was standing in the line of trees. When the re-enactor passed him, he didn't move or say a word and immediately disappeared.

Confederate re-enactor soldiers preparing for battle, located on Starkweather's Hill, Perryville, Kentucky.

The Union Regiment

On the 125th Anniversary of the battle, some of the Union and Confederate re-enactors were awakened by noise coming from the adjacent field across from the Benton-White Road. They approached the field and noticed a Union regiment drilling in the middle of the night. It was a bright moonlit night and the flags of the Union regiment were waving in the wind. All present watching this grand spectacle was amazed how well this Union regiment executed its moves. The commander of the Union regiment barked out his orders. But the re-enactors were a little upset by being awakened at night. Most of the re-enactors watching the Union regiment wondered why they couldn't have drilled with the rest of the other regiments in the morning.

The next day, at officer's call, the Union and Confederate regiment commanders asked, "Who was the Union regiment that was drilling so well last night?"

All the commanders looked at each other, and each said it wasn't them.

Union soldiers march past where the 1st Michigan Light Artillery, Coldwater, fought at Perryville. The ghost of a Union soldier and spectral cannons appear on the same spot.

The Ghost on the Old Lebanon Road

On a November evening near dusk, two couples were traveling north on the old Lebanon Road. They just started to drive the last wide curve before the road straightens out and leads into Perryville when they saw a stranger standing along the road amid the gathering mist. He had the long hollow stare as if someone in a trance.

One of the occupants in the car, who studied the battle of Perryville thoroughly, noticed something amazing about this man standing by the road. He was wearing a Confederate infantryman's coat, cap, and gear. Realizing what an amazing sight they had just seen, the driver of the car quickly slammed on his brakes, wheeled his car around, and sped back to the spot where the Confederate soldier was standing. But the Infantryman had already vanished into thin air.

The Disappearing Cemetery

Several years ago several Union re-enactors decided to walk the battlefield at night. They walked the Benton White Road and came to the intersection of the Hays-Mays Road. They took the Hays-Mays Road and approached the Russell House. The Russell House no longer exists, but the foundation of the house remains.

As the re-enactors approached the house, the field became extremely quiet. Not a sound was heard. No crickets, no frogs, and nothing but dead silence.

Soon one of the Union re-enactors felt as if someone was watching him. Once the area of the field around the Russell House had been cleared, the crickets again started to chirp.

A story related to the Russell House occurred one night when several re-enactors walked along the same stretch of road. It was a warm October evening and sweat began to drip off the foreheads of the re-enactors, since wearing wool uniforms and multi-layered dresses can become quite warm. But as they approached the tops of some of the hills, the air became quite still and the temperature quickly dropped.

The Union re-enactors soon saw their breath. This happened on several hilltops. As they looked out at the fields, there were small clumps of fog that moved across the field as if small companies of soldiers were rushing to the battle lines. All the clumps of fog were heading towards the Bottom's House. It was an eerie sight.

Another story about the Hays-Mays Road involves several re-enactors walking the road. Along the road there is a small cemetery called the White Chapel Cemetery. One of the lady re-enactors looked at the many tombstones in the cemetery. Since she loved genealogy, she remarked at the age of the some of the headstones. There was a male re-enactor who studied genealogy. He agreed that they should come back the following day to research names on the tombstones.

The next day came and it was forgotten. The re-enactors were too busy preparing for the day's re-creation of the battle to return to the same area where they saw the tombstones. But the next year, the same re-enactors decided to walk the Hays-Mays Road. When they came to the cemetery, to their amazement and shock, there were no graves, and no tombstones. The next day when it was light out, the re-enactors went to the cemetery. They found no graves except two. But these burials occurred in 1996 and none of the property had been disturbed.

Yet another story related to the Russell House and the Hays-Mays Road was told by several Union and Confederate soldiers who also decided to walk the Hays-Mays Road late at night. They heard about the stories of ghosts and weird occurrences that had taken place and decided to check out the road.

They did not believe in ghosts but decided to try their luck at ghost hunting. While walking along the road, they had become separated from the main group of re-enactors and were several yards behind the rest of the group. All of a sudden, the whole area lit up and it almost seemed like it was daylight. The occurrence lasted only for a couple of seconds and then it became night again.

The re-enactors stood in shock. They began to ask themselves if they really saw what they thought they had experienced. The re-enactors tried to come up with explanations. They figured maybe it was the lights of an airplane that lit up their area. But this could not have been the explanation because there were no planes in the sky. They tried to explain it away by saying that it was a car's headlights but there were no cars on the road in front of them and no car could have lit up the whole area. Perhaps these re-enactors walked into a rip in the orderly fabric of time and found daylight of 1862 for a few seconds. Or maybe the past pushed forward into the present time, leaving these living souls amazed by the vision of a world long past.

The Ghost Cannons and the Lone Infantryman

On the 140th Anniversary of the Battle of Perryville, several re-enactors decided to walk the Hay-Mays Road leading towards the Bottom's House. They approached the hill where the 1st Michigan Light Artillery from Coldwater, Michigan, fought on October 8th. One of the re-enactors pointed to the silhouette of a Union infantryman carrying his rifle and wearing all his gear. The soldier was crossing between several large cannons. One of the re-enactors decided to sprint up the hill to see if this lone Union infantryman was real. As he approached the soldier, he noticed that he could see him walk across the pavement but he made no sound. The soldier continued to walk from one side of the pavement to the other. As he reached the other side, to the amazement of the re-enactor, the soldier approached a barb wired fence and walked right though it! The re-enactor was in shock as he watched the lone Union infantryman fade into the darkness. His fellow re-enactors caught up with him and the shocked re-enactor relayed his story—excited and scared at the sighting.

The next day, the re-enactors who experienced the lone Union infantryman helped set up cannons on the exact same site where they saw the apparition. As they unlimbered the cannons from their trailers for the upcoming battle, one of the re-enactors turned and noticed that there was only one cannon on the hill. The re-enactor quickly realized that when they had approached the hill the previous night, the lone Union infantryman had walked in between several cannons on the ridge, not just one single cannon. Just at that moment all the re-enactors that were on that fateful walk realized that they had seen not only the lone Union infantryman but experienced the vision of multiple cannons.

It may be that a lone Union sentry still protects the cannons. And despite the passage of our earthly time, the guns of the 1st Michigan Light Artillery are forever poised to fight the oncoming Confederate soldiers and the shells of the Confederate guns of the 5th Louisiana Battery.

The Confederate Drummer Boy

During one of the national re-enactments, several Union and Confederate artillery units decided to camp behind the Civil War Museum on the battlefield. The Museum is located near the Confederate mass grave and monument to the Confederate dead at Perryville. The area is near a flat field before the steep incline runs towards Starkweather's hill.

On a crisp, chilly, early Sunday morning at the re-enactors camp site, as dew clung to the tents, the camp cook started breakfast for the men, women, and children in camp. She stoked the embers to start a fire in the fire pit. As the flames arose and the embers started to glow red, she was busy preparing the eggs, bacon, biscuits, and gravy. As the smells of bacon filled the air, the other members of the unit arose out of their slumber. Many of the fellow re-enactors got out their coffee pots and continued a tradition carried down since the dawn of modern warfare—the making of a pot of coffee. More and more re-enactors gathered around the campfire to shake off the cold.

While the re-enactors sat around the campfire, they began to discuss with the camp historian about the battle and the area where they were camped. As they were talking, a boy of around twelve or thirteen years of age sat down with the re-enactors. He wore a Confederate gray kepi, gray wool pants, and a white muslin shirt. No one at the time questioned who he was and most assumed he was with one of the surrounding units who just wanted to sit down near the warm fire. Nothing of importance set the boy apart from any other boy, except that, before the breakfast, he said absolutely nothing during the conversations between the other re-enactors. He mostly seemed to just sit and stare at the fire.

When breakfast was ready and the gravy, eggs, and the coffee were just right, the camp cook told all the re-enactors to get their plates and cups and get ready to feast on the bountiful food. The Confederate boy got up and stood in line with the other re-enactors. The camp cook noticed the young boy without a plate and cup and suggested that he grab one of the extra plates. Amazingly, none of the re-enactors noticed him with a plate and after the re-enactors started to eat, they noticed that the Confederate boy never had anything to eat. He just disappeared. Most re-enactors assumed he just walked away.

After the re-enactment was over many of the re-enactors began to talk about the mysterious Confederate boy who never said or ate anything. They asked the other re-enacting units if they knew who the boy was and

At one of the national re-enactments, at night, a ghost Union regiment was seen drilling in the fields at Perryville.

where he belonged. No one remembered seeing him in the other camps nor knew him.

The re-enactors in the units visited by the young Confederate boy decided to enter the museum to see if someone inside had seen the young stranger. The museum staff mentioned that many of the tourists who visited the museum when there was no re-enactment mentioned seeing a young Confederate boy walking around the museum. Who could this young Confederate boy be? Is he one of the many of thousands of young men who died during the battle of Perryville? Many young boys caught up in the fever of war decided to join the Union or Confederacy to become drummer boys. They beat out the orders on their drums and many times were in the thick of battle. Unfortunately, many of them were severely wounded or killed, asking for their mothers as they breathed their last breath upon the earth.

During a recent re-enactment, several re-enactors walked the battlefield at night. Two of the Union soldier re-enactors broke away from the rest of the group and walked the Hays-Mays Road by themselves. While walking along the road both men witnessed the night turning into daylight for about two or three seconds. Both of the men stopped in their tracks, bewildered at what just happened to them. Both of the men tried to explain the event. They thought maybe a helicopter or plane had turned on their spotlights but again, there were no planes or helicopters that could be heard. The two men finally came to the conclusion they could not explain the night turning to day. Possibly both men had walked into residual haunting.

Operations Have Not Ceased

Beautiful Maple Hill Manor Bed and Breakfast is owned and operated by Todd Allen and Tyler Horton. Maple Hill Manor is located on the Perryville Road in Washington County, Kentucky, not more than fifteen miles from the Perryville Battlefield and close to the county seat, Springfield. Like many local homes, this Greek Revival Plantation was used as a field hospital for surgery on the soldiers injured at Perryville.

Back in 1848, Thomas I. McElroy supervised construction of what was to become a perfect gift to his youthful bride, Sarah Maxwell. Seventeen-year-old Sarah likely toured the construction site in happy anticipation of moving in. She would have witnessed craftsmen forming the details of Italianate architectural design such as fourteen-foot high ceilings, two-and-a-half-foot cornices, and arched windowpanes. The structure was brick and inside hardwood floors shone and a cherry wood banister curved to the second floor.

Reportedly, it was just a week after Sarah's birthday in 1851 when they moved into their spacious home. Thomas McElroy owned slaves and there are some who report seeing the shackles hanging still on the stone walled cellar basement. Slaves labored on this six hundred acre plantation while life proceeded in relative order until the summer of 1862 when rumor of passing armies flooded the Bluegrass. After the terrible Battle of Perryville in October that fall, families opened their homes either willingly or reluctantly to help the armies deal with the countless wounded soldiers.

I imagine it was stressful, if not traumatic, for family members to witness the battle surgeons struggle to amputate and operate to save soldiers. Sara McElroy would have been about twenty-eight years old and if her children were there to watch in horror, they may have seen stacks of amputated limbs outside the house. Slaves likely worked diligently, bringing water and bandages and trying in vain to scrub bloodstains from the floors.

I visited Maple Hill Manor for their ghost tour on October 21 & 22 in 2005. I enjoyed staying there in early 2003 and the Innkeepers asked me to return to be a part of their ghost tours to tell their guests about the ghosts at Shakertown. Todd walked us throughout their home from kitchen to cellar to first and second floor bedrooms. He talked about odd experiences from the previous owners and tales that their guests reported. Evidently, Maple Hill Manor houses more that a few ghosts, from a five-year-old boy to a female African slave to Civil War surgeons.

I took my tape recorder and stood open-mouthed as the other guests and I heard tale after tale of the sounds and scents of their haunted Bed and Breakfast. Folks have smelled a rose scent and cigar smoke, too—both without rational explanation or visible source. Maple Hill Manor attracted the attention of paranormal investigators, including Lexington's Patti Starr and Kentucky author Lynwood Montell. His *Haunted Houses and Family Ghosts of Kentucky* has numerous pages devoted to Maple Hill Manor. (See in his book the story #126 on pages 147 and following).

While we walked through the dark home and guests took digital photos (yes some folks captured photographic anomalies), Todd told us about kitchen cabinet doors and drawers discovered pulled out. He also pointed out a section of the banister toward the second floor landing which is not original. Evidently, a five-year-old boy, just days after his birthday, fell from there and did not recover from his injuries. The previous owners talked about hearing talking or mysterious music; when they looked for the source, it was never found. Guests report a presence in one room that seems to be a protective slave woman named "Mamma Ann". I have an unusual digital picture that shows a faint shape in that room. It seems to be leaning toward our tour guide!

In another room, the water has been found running on its own. The owners maintained that they are unwilling to take guests to tour the cellar as the spirits of the slaves are not happy and wish to be left alone. Todd talked about hearing chains rattle.

But it is a second floor guest room toward the back on the south side that evidently was used to deal with the wounded soldiers from Perryville. A number of guests reported waking to a nightmare in which they are the soldier under the saw or knife of the Union surgeon.

Todd reported that people in that room dream "you are being cut." Although these visions appear to unwilling witnesses and despite the unpleasant nature of a long-ago life and death struggle, we in our practical world must admit that the Civil War has never really ceased.

Maple Hill Manor Bed and Breakfast, Springfield, Kentucky. *Courtesy of Todd Allen.*

The Nurse is Still On Duty

The Homestead Bed and Breakfast was another historic home which saw service not only treating the soldiers after the Battle of Perryville but where soldiers were quartered for some time. The Homestead sits just outside Bardstown, Kentucky, on the Bloomfield Road. It is a lovely place to stay and owner and hostess, Joanne Hobbs, readily regales visitors with tales of ghostly activity, which happened to both she and her guests.

Joanne reports that the Homestead was built in the late 1700s. But when Joanne Hobbs moved to Bardstown and bought an interesting old home, no one, including the seller, knew what amazing architecture lay beneath the centuries of remodeling and additions. Joanne and the renovators diligently endeavored to rebuild that which had been fallen down, covered up, broken or taken over by raccoons. One of her workers found massive poplar logs. Slaves had hewn these logs, some 16-18 inches square, for the original building. A slave wing was added later; today you can see that section which is now a kitchen. Brick floors complemented by an open vault to the second story highlight the kitchen, which shows, on the west wall, a plaque with the names of the slaves.

History is embedded within the home itself, and also in the land at the Homestead. It was the only stage stop and home from Bloomfield to Bardstown. The Union Army stopped and stayed, using one of the many springs on the property, and no doubt quartering both inside and on the grounds. As a Historic Kentucky Landmark, the Homestead carries layers of feeling, both dignified and mysterious. Joanne took me on a walkabout tour, showing me the downstairs parlors, game room, and bedrooms upstairs.

As we walked through this home I felt a very real sense of history and also an unmistakable presence. But according to Joanne, and for many who visit, the Homestead hosts a number of spirits. I spent the night in a guest room on the second floor, which faced the Bloomfield Road. I felt I was not

The Homestead Bed and Breakfast, Bardstown, Kentucky. *Photo by Thomas Freese.*

alone but, needing a good night's sleep, I pleaded in my telepathic thoughts to the spirits that I wanted to be left alone to get some rest.

After breakfast, I explored the grounds, walking out the whistle path to see the stone cellar and milk house. I wandered toward the driveway, past a tree that is much older that the Homestead itself. There is a little stream and an arched wooden bridge over the spring-fed stream. Behind the house, I found a set of a dozen gravestones propped up with a metal rod behind each one. Joanne said that the headstones had been removed from their original site, farther back on the property. When she found the facedown gravestones, she felt the need to honor those spirits and, not knowing the original graveyard location, propped them up with metal bars in an orderly row in the backyard. We chatted out in the warm sunshine, as Joanne plucked hard pears off the tree, tossing them to the chickens.

Joanne told me about her resident ghosts.

"The ghosts chase my dog Daisy. I believe there are mostly all slave spirits here. The electrician who did remodeling work was not a believer in ghosts. But he kept having problems, which he fixed, and then they were unfixed by the ghosts. Then he had to fix them again. He said,

'Something's going on in here.'

Homestead Bed and Breakfast front porch. *Photo by Thomas Freese.*

"They had a terrible time with the telephone line. I couldn't call the phone company to report that it was a problem with ghosts. One day I was brushing my teeth, leaning over the sink. I heard a faraway sound of a phone ringing. So I turned off the running water but then I didn't hear the ringing. I resumed brushing my teeth, and again I heard the ringing sound. Then it sounded as if it was coming from the drain. Five minutes later the phone really did ring downstairs but only from downstairs. I finally took the phone out of the game room.

"I've always had trouble with smoke detectors here. It's been a nightmare! I had trouble with one smoke detector on the landing. One afternoon it started beeping and someone said please put in a new battery. I put in a new battery but thirty minutes later, it again started beeping. It started and quit on an off until by 10:30 I had enough and I turned off the electrical breaker switch. But even then it went to beeping again.

"The electrician came over with his wife Becky. They brought a brand new smoke detector. Becky picked up Daisy, who was shaking like a leaf. We were three puzzled people with a very scared dog.

"Becky said, 'There's somebody blowing on my neck.'

"We took out that battery and put in a *new* battery. While we all stood there, with the electrician holding the old detector, which no longer had a battery—it started beeping!

"Then the pest technician came and he always seemed a bit leery of the place. He knew there were ghosts. I have an old wagon outside filled in season with flowers. There is also a birdhouse that was leaning against the shop wall. Once, the pest technician was working in the side yard, putting termite traps in the ground in the flowerbed. The man came running up to me, shaking, and said, 'You've got to come out here. I can't believe what's going on. You've got to come out here to see this!'

"When I followed him outside I saw the wagon was flipped over. Then a second later the birdhouse fell over. There was no one else around and no wind."

Joanne had paranormal investigator Patti Starr come and see what spirits are present at the Homestead. Patti brings dowsing rods to communicate with the ghosts and she also takes video or still digital images.

Joanne:

"Patti suggested that I walk out to the porch and put out my hand. Some kind of white thing showed up by the window. It looked like a nurse, kneeling down. Patti asked, 'Are you the protector spirit?' The ghost nurse said she was, that she helped care for thirty-four Civil War soldiers who were injured and quartered in that room.

"Since there were only three houses between the towns of Bloomfield and Bardstown, the Union soldiers set up camp at the Homestead. Those three homes each had water springs. One of the family members from this house was a big drinker. His name was Henry Nicholls, and when he was drafted, he didn't want to fight in the Civil War. The night before he was to appear before the draft board, he drank castor and mineral oil. The next day at his military physical, they noted his 'consumption of the bowels' and allowed him to pay someone else $5,000 to go fight in his place."

What a terrible conflict was the Civil War, where a wealthy man would pay in excess of, in today's dollars, $50,000 to avoid facing bayonet, bullet, and cannon fire.

Phantom Artillery Crew

Terrell Bryant, Re-enactor since 1989

On a Saturday evening, close to the Battle of Perryville, on the 140th anniversary of the battle, we were at Perryville, Kentucky, in the battlefield by the monument in the middle of the park. The artillery was supposed to be doing a night firing. A nighttime demonstration shows the spectators what the night shooting looked like. Private Greg Elden and my brother in law Travis Casto and I sat on the bench looking up toward what they call Heart Attack Hill. This hill has a permanent cannon placement on top the hill for spectators. Folks can go on up there and see where the cannons were placed and get a feel for the perspective of the artillery.

The sun always sets in behind the hills. So we thought that the crew members we saw were the artillery re-enactors doing a night firing. We sat and watched the men go through the motions. The sun set behind the hill and backlit the sky and the artillery crew.

Union artillery located at the sinkhole prepares to meet oncoming Confederate troops.

We watched this cannon crew going through maneuvers. It looked like they were loading and shooting the cannons. But they weren't really shooting anything—we didn't hear or see the cannon go off. They were just going through the maneuvers. They were just practicing to get ready for shooting.

We watched them go through the maneuvers a couple of times when we saw a group of spectators who walked up the hill toward the cannons. We watched them get up to the cannons and then the cannon crew just vanished in midair.

So they walked around like they had never seen anything. But we three, and everybody standing around us, had sat there and watched these guys and saw how good they looked because they looked like they were right there doing it.

I think the ghosts see the re-enactors in uniform and they feel like it's a little easier to let down their guard. I think re-enactors might feel like they have a better insight to what the soldier's life was like. They try to live life like the soldiers did back in the Civil War. The re-enactors try to honor the sacrifices that the soldiers made. So I think they let down their guard and let you see a little bit of their life and what they were doing.

Ghost Soldiers Were All Around Us

Prior to that, Scott Hearst and another soldier and I were in the 5th Kentucky. We belonged to the Tennessee Valley Battalion with Travis Casto. We were sent up early on Wednesday, prior to the battle that weekend. We set up the advance guard for the Battalion. We set up markers and stuff to make sure nobody else camped out in that area.

We were in the woods there on the left hand side of the park. There was nobody else up there in the park except us three and the park ranger. When we checked in with him earlier that day, he assured us that there was nobody else in the park.

We went there and got our little fire going. It started getting dark and we heard coyotes barking. All the food we had was packed in our knapsacks.

I told the other guys "Let's take our food and scoot it up closer to the fire. That'll keep the coyotes from getting into it in the middle of the night."

After we moved our food by the fire, we sat back and looked at the stars over the tree tops. All the sudden, a nice little breeze blew up. It was warm. Then we noticed a fog, which came up out of the sinkhole. The fog covered the entire valley where the sinkhole was and came around to the little patch of woods where we were camped. But the fog never came into the woods; it stayed out over the fields.

Union soldiers march towards the sinkhole, Perryville Battle reenactment.

Union soldiers prepare for Confederate forces at the sinkhole, Perryville Battle reenactment.

We continued, despite some fog, to look past the trees at the stars and we were surprised to hear what sounded like an officer calling out a command. We heard him holler although we couldn't make out exactly what he said. Right after he called out, we heard another man repeat the command as if it was the first sergeant or colonel repeating the command back to the captain. Then it fell silent for a while.

A little bit later, I asked my buddies "Did you all hear that?"

They answered back, "Yeah, we heard it!"

I said "Well, there isn't supposed to be anyone else here in the park, just us."

We sat there for about fifteen minutes in silence, not hearing anything else. We each thought about the reality or unreality of what we heard. I wondered *maybe we heard somebody else on the next farm over?* We looked at the stars in the quiet night.

Not much later, we heard a bunch of horses running alongside the woods. It sounded like cavalry horses coming close to our camp. Then we heard the group of horses turn and run down to the sinkhole. We couldn't see a thing but it sounded like there were twenty or more horses running in the field. We heard them run at a full gallop until they turned and went left toward the sinkhole.

Scott sat up and demanded "Did you all hear those horses?"

I agreed "Yeah, I heard them but there should be nobody else in here unless somebody's doing a night maneuver."

Sometimes cavalry re-enactors camp out on land adjacent to the park and just ride in. So we talked about how it could be someone like that. We got to talking about the weekend jobs we had to do and we heard again down at the sinkhole an officer shout a command. I heard a second soldier repeat the command and then we heard rifles shooting. It sounded like a whole company of soldiers firing off in the valley.

All three of us jumped up and looked out from our camp. We didn't see anything! Our eyes must have looked as big as half dollars as we strained to see through the black night and wondered what was happening. We couldn't see down through the fog. About five minutes later, we heard one soldier yell a command and another guy repeated it and a volley of shots went off again!

Now the park ranger assured us that we were the only three in the park so our nerves started to get frayed. It was late in the evening and we tried to lie down again to try to sleep. We curled up in our blankets but not one of us could get to sleep. We talked again and again about what we heard on that old battlefield. We went over the events and sounds in our heads and tried to make sense of the mysterious commands, rifle volleys, fog, and cavalry charge. Surely we experienced all that the haunted Perryville Battlefield offered to solitary mortals encamped for the night.

About an hour then passed and above us we heard the footsteps of soldiers coming though the woods. We clearly heard them stepping on tree branches and leaves. It sounded like there was a whole line of phantom soldiers. We all rolled over on our stomach as the sound of the marching army moved toward us. I pulled out my bayonet and stuck it in the ground in front of me to have something to try and defend us.

They continued to march through the woods toward us, getting closer and closer. We literally heard their tin cups scrape the trees and water sloshing in canteens. When the ghost company got to within fifteen or twenty yards from

Union infantry march out on the battlefield.

us, all the sound just ceased. We never heard anything else. We lay awake the rest of that dark morning until dawn, hearing not another ghostly sound. We were all tore up and we couldn't get back to sleep.

The next day, we walked over to speak to the park ranger. We asked him if any of the other re-enactor units had come into the park at night. He told us that there were no other re-enactors in the park at the time.

Call to the Line

The next evening, Thursday night, some of the other men from our Battalion joined us. We tied our ponchos to the trees as the rain was coming in. One of our guys, Barry, told us the next day that while he slept he was suddenly awakened by somebody pulling at his pants leg. He raised himself up to look and saw a Confederate soldier squatted down with his rifle leaning up on him.

The Southern soldier said, "He wants you up there."

The ghost pointed outside the tent. Barry followed his line of sight, looking out of his tent, but saw no one.

The ghost Confederate repeated, "He wants you up there."

Barry again saw no one outside and turned back around to face the ghost. As rain fell outside, Barry saw water dripping down the brim of the soldier's hat.

The ghost then leaned forward to hand his rifle and said, "Here you might need this."

Barry looked one more time outside the tent to try to make sense of this impossible specter and when his eyes returned to his tent inside, the ghost had vanished.

He climbed out of his sleeping blanket to look around the tent. There was not a soul in sight, not even the back of a prankster walking away.

Ghostly Vision

John Wiedeburg
About ten years ago I was part of the re-enactment at Perryville Battlefield. It was close to the actual battle anniversary. It was one of the National re-enactments.

As I looked out over the battlefield I was surprised to notice the air start to shimmer. Then I found myself looking at the images of battle, not our re-enactment but of the actual battle, which occurred in 1862. There were only eight of us who saw this vision of the past. Spectators walked around us or through the same space as the battle but they didn't notice the vision.

We asked others around us, "Don't you see them?"

They answered, "Do we see what?!"

A re-enactment of Union soldiers holding off Donelson's brigade assault, Perryville Battle reenactment.

And we had headaches from the vortex, from this wavy view of the past. We saw the actual soldiers fighting although their figures appeared hazy to us.

Talking With the Dead

Janine Bennett

John [Wiedeburg] and I were at the Perryville Battlefield about ten years ago. He went into the restroom by the parking lot.

A Confederate cavalry soldier came up and asked, "Where is my horse?"

He was just a few feet away and I could see into his eyes.

I pointed north toward the hill. The soldier started walking in that direction but after a half dozen steps just disappeared into thin air. I thought he was real, that he was a re-enactor.

Ghostly Soldier Came Home with Us

Janine Bennett

We were at the national re-enactment at Perryville, Kentucky, in 2001. That was when I saw the ghost cavalryman. I also saw another Confederate soldier who I thought was real. I thought he was a lonely re-enactor as I walked near him. He sat on a tree stump looking homesick or sad. He had short hair and medium build.

I asked him, "What's wrong?"

He just shrugged his shoulders and looked down.

I asked him, "I'm going to cook some food. Would you like a steak?"

He answered "Yes" but when I finished cooking, he was nowhere to be found.

But John and I hadn't seen the last of him. We returned home to Louisville and we quickly had some odd things happen that led us to believe that the lonely Rebel ghost wanted to stay with us.

John bought a musical CD from the re-enactment. It had reproduced period band music and was performed completely in concert with Northern or Union songs. Evidently our Confederate soldier ghost didn't like the tunes. John watched in shock as the CD player opened, the disc floated up into the air and split in half.

John told the ghost, "Don't do that again!"

We felt that his name was Zach and he liked our house cats. In fact, there was more than one occasion when we saw our Siamese cat go through the house floating in thin air as if being carried on the arm of someone—an invisible someone.

It seemed like Zach liked to play pranks on us. He made some of John's money disappear only to bring it out of hiding later. He was active now and then until we moved to our new house. But just as we packed up and took our boxes to the truck, he gave us one more show. There was a short bamboo stick that lay on the ground in front. As we both watched in amazement, the stick stood upright and started hopping back and forth. We simply walked away after five minutes!

Ghost Soldier on Our Farm

John Wiedeburg

This happened back in the later 1950s. I'd say it was in 1958 when my family had a 260-acre farm in Sinking Fork, Oldham County, Kentucky. My older brother and my sister helped to get the cattle back to the barn one time when they saw a Civil War soldier. Their names are Roger and Sugarpie.

As they went along through the woods, they came upon a Confederate soldier who sat on a tree stump. He had a "kepi" cap and smoked a pipe. They said he didn't say anything at all. He just calmly puffed on the pipe and watched them go by. They told me he had a beard. Then when they looked back, he was gone. They felt quite spooked by the sighting.

The Ghostly Confederate Cavalrymen

Several years ago, a group of Civil War re-enactors decided to walk at night on the Hays-Mays road leading to the Bottom's House. Several of the male re-enactors had already seen the Bottom's House and decided to stay back at the area where the 1st Michigan Light Artillery took position during the battle, while the lady re-enactors decided to walk to the Bottom's house. After the ladies saw the Bottom's House, they headed back up the long hill to where the rest of the group waited for them. As they walked up the hill, two Confederate cavalrymen rode at a slow pace past them. One of the Confederate cavalrymen had a beautiful white horse. On top of the cavalryman's head was a hat with a flowing black ostrich plume cascading down the side of the hat.

One of the ladies asked in a humorous manner, "Are you real or are you a ghost?"

Both men continued to ride their horses without responding to her question. The cavalrymen headed toward the area where the rest of the re-enactors were waiting for the lady re-enactors. The women watched the Confederate cavalrymen ride up the hill but they could not keep up with the horses.

The lady re-enactors caught up with the rest of the group and asked the male re-enactors if they saw the Confederate cavalrymen. The male re-enactors said that they heard horse hooves hitting the ground and the clanking of a cavalry saber hitting the side of the saddle but did not see the Confederate cavalrymen. The Confederate cavalrymen vanished by the time they arrived at the top of the hill.

Shaker Village and the Civil War

In 1774, Mother Ann Lee and a small band of converts came from England to New York. She was the founder of Shakerism in America. On August 15, 1805, Elisha Thomas and Samuel and Henry Banta attended a Revival at Concord, Bourbon County, Kentucky. They were converted by missionaries to accept the doctrine of United Society of Believers in Christ's Second Coming. Thomas and the Bantas decided to introduce Shakerism to Mercer County, Kentucky. In 1806, the new Believers located their community at Shawnee Run on Thomas's farm near each other for religious worship and protection. On December 3, 1806, forty-four converts signed the first family covenant and agreed to mutual support and common property ownership. In 1808, the forty-four members built their first meetinghouse.

The Shaker 1820 Meeting House, Pleasant Hill, Mercer County, Kentucky. *Photo by Thomas Freese.*

The name Shaker came from vigorous worship practice. The Shakers were devout, orderly, and followed celibacy. They excelled in architecture, farming, and inventions. They also became known for their seed business and furniture making. At the community's height, there were five hundred members and they expanded their farm to five thousand acres of land with twenty-five miles of rock fences.

Completed in 1839, the Lexington-Harrodsburg-Perryville Turnpike ran through the center of Shaker Village at Pleasant Hill. The road became part of interstate Zanesville (Ohio)-Florence (Alabama) mail stage route. The turnpike brought the reclusive Shakers communication and trade but the road also brought Union and Confederate soldiers into their community. On July 13, 1862, the Shakers hid their horses from Confederate General John Hunt Morgan's cavalry, when his men rode through their community but Morgan told his men not to trespass or molest the Shakers out of respect for their religion. After the Battle of Perryville, on October 11, 1862, Morgan and his men retreated through their village and the Shakers had not forgotten Morgan's good treatment of their members on his last trip and treated his men to a feast.

By 1877, the stage coaches on the Lexington-Harrodsburg-Perryville Turnpike ceased to operate along the route and, by 1910, the last twelve members deeded their land to a private citizen, and in return, he cared for them during their remaining years. By 1923, Sister Mary Settles died at Shaker Village. She was the last Shaker to live in the community. In 1961, the restoration began on Shaker Village at Pleasant Hill, and the state has a shining jewel of a community where visitors can relive the Believers' dream of peace.

All of the Shaker villages were dramatically affected by the Civil War, some more directly than others. Pleasant Hill in Mercer County, Kentucky, saw a direct impact as a result of both the Battle of Perryville and due to other troop movements of the opposing forces. Shaker journals report at least one soldier being buried in their cemetery while the pacifist Shaker brethren struggled to remain neutral. This was a difficult task however as both Federal and Confederate forces moved through the Shaker land from their Kentucky River landing, along their roads and even via the countryside.

Confederate regular forces as well as guerilla elements asked or demanded water, food, livestock, and wagons. Snipers shot at riverboat traffic and the Union forces at one point seized the Shaker landing, even sinking ferryboats to prevent John Hunt Morgan from crossing the Kentucky River. On a prior trip, John Hunt Morgan and his forces were fed by the Pleasant Hill Shakers. Appeasing the powerful of the world sometimes brought protective favor at a later date.

The Shaker journals from Pleasant Hill talk about how they heard the sounds of the cannons at Perryville, just seven miles away. The wounded straggled through their village and the Shakers depleted their resources,

Shaker Cemetery at Pleasant Hill, Kentucky. *Photo by Thomas Freese.*

time, and much care to assist those soldiers. One Shaker wrote: "We have kept our horses and wagons concealed except those that necessity compelled us to use. We also secreted most of our valuables, such as cloth, flour, preserves, etc.

"October 24, 1862: William Henry Outlaw, a paroled Confederate soldier from Georgia died here and three of his brethren followed his remains to our humble Cemetery where he was decently interred. Thomas Shain, William Runyon and William Maire went to Perryville to carry some sanitary supplies to the sick and wounded soldiers." (From *Ye Olde Shaker Bells*, pg. 63, Nancy Lewis Greene)

Another entry in 1862: "But the most important events have transpired in the political and military world that ever occurred on this continent, or perhaps any other, since the expulsion of the Arch Fiend from the Empyrean of Jehovah. That most unholy and fratricidal war which has been waged in this disturbed century, has raged with the fury of the Beast, and with capricious fortune, and has hurled its thousands into the dark abyss below. It has emphatically been the year of battles and human slaughter." F. W. Kepart (*Pleasant Hill Shakers in the Civil War 1861-1865*, 1988)

Since the Shakers dealt firsthand with the trauma of the Civil War, it would be quite possible that the indelible impression stayed with them even as they crossed over into the spirit realm. There is no doubt for many employees of and visitors to Pleasant Hill that the Shaker ghosts are active and interactive with the living. Please find my first book, *Shaker Ghost Stories from Pleasant Hill,* Kentucky (2005), which gives detailed testimonies from over sixty interviews as to the haunting at Shakertown.

In fact Civil, War re-enactors regularly encamp at the restored Shaker village. They experienced ghostly events and perhaps these spirits were the Shakers, feeling restless or uncomfortable with these soldiers "returning" to their beloved village.

Ninth Massachusetts Infantry. *Courtesy Library of Congress.*

One of the Confederate re-enactors was giving tours of the Civil War encampment in June 1998. I chatted with the re-enactors about their camping weekend, and I eventually got around to asking them about Shaker ghosts. I figured that they were the rugged kind of guys who probably looked at life realistically, and that they likely didn't believe in ghosts. But the re-enactors immediately spoke up about something that had happened that weekend. They had been in the Old Ministry's Shop. They had closed the back door, but they found it kept popping open.

The men would yell, "Come on in!"

Then they'd get up and shut the door. This happened four times.

One man and his fellow re-enactors from the 4th Kentucky Volunteer Infantry had a Shaker experience there.

He said, "Two years ago we held our Civil War encampment. We were driven into the West Family Dwelling to spend the night because of rain. We were upstairs and in the back room. Well, the men couldn't find a switch to turn off the lights." The light bulbs are in reproduction wooden wall sconces.

"The guys unscrewed all the bulbs so we'd be able to sleep better without the lights being on."

One light bulb came on, so they unscrewed it again. Then *two* bulbs came on and they got up and unscrewed those again. They actually then took out those two bulbs, completely removing them from their sockets. Then another one came on! In the course of an hour, four bulbs came on, just as quickly as they could get them unscrewed. And the door to the restroom swung open as they unscrewed the last light bulb.

Outside the Meetinghouse, on the village road, there have been a few sightings. The village pike was actually US Highway 68 until the creators of the restored Shakertown wisely diverted the highway farther south. It is now a peaceful village lane lined by trees. Visitors find Pleasant Hill employees demonstrating crafts in the shade of the trees. Soldiers from the bi-annual Civil War encampment march down the pike, much like the traveling armies of the Union and Confederate forces did in the nineteenth century. Visitors ride horse-drawn wagons on their Shakertown tour. It is common to see the Pleasant Hill employees, dressed in Shaker attire, walking to work or back from lunch.

One employee told of an interesting event that occurred during the 1996 Civil War reenactment. He said that many of the men who were portraying the soldiers knew very little about the Shakers and their type of worship. They had placed an overnight sentry at the corner of the Centre Family Dwelling, across from the Meetinghouse. Another employee checked on them the next day.

The first employee said, "These guys were terrified!"

The sentries asked, "What the heck was going on last night? At three in the morning, we heard the most awful racket coming from the Meetinghouse. We heard people clapping their hands and singing; they were stomping and shouting too!"

The employee said that they were very serious about the truth of their experience.

"They discovered how the Shakers worshipped."

Camp Boone,
Tennessee

"The first few easy going, quiet days of our new camp brought vividly to mind our early soldier experiences of camps Boone and Burnett, minus of course, the abundant comforts of those camps and the sanguine buds of hope which had been nipped by many killing frosts since that rosy summer when our hearts held but one fear, and that was that 'the wayward sisters would be allowed to depart in peace,' before we had met our enemy on the field of battle. Now we all knew how often we had met him and what became of it."[1]

This was written by a member of the Lewis Kentucky Brigade.

Before the first shots were fired on Fort Sumter, in the Charleston Harbor in April 1861, Kentucky was a border state that was very nationalistic in sentiment but very Pro-Southern economically. Kentucky statesmen were hoping that the Commonwealth of Kentucky would work out a compromise. When the war broke out, Kentucky's governor refused to honor the newly elected President Lincoln's call for 75,000 troops. Sentiments among Kentuckians ran high. Each side hoped that the legislature would pass a vote on which side the state would take a stand, whether it was Union or Confederate. But Kentucky opted for neutrality.

On May 20, 1861, Kentucky voted to remain neutral. This did not stop both parties from preparing for war. Both sides set up camps of instruction and drill. Some of the members of the Kentucky legislature who were Pro-Southern started to organize themselves into companies and in May left the State and marched to Virginia, where they were recognized by General Johnston. They were officially recognized as the First Regiment Kentucky Volunteer Infantry. Camp Joe Holt was established near Jeffersonville, Indiana, and recruiting officers were sent into Kentucky to encourage the men of the area to battle the Union forces. Rallies were held, while bands played "Dixie." Union recruiting centers also were in the same area and they would play the "Star Spangled Banner."

In June 1861, Colonel William Temp Withers, Colonel Robert A. Johnson, and Colonel James W. Hewitt determined to recruit a regiment for the Southern army. They were aided by some of the wealthiest and influential citizens in Louisville, Kentucky, who spent their own money providing the new Kentucky Confederate troops with transportation and supplies. Authority was given by the Confederate government to establish a recruiting station that had easy access to Kentucky and to organize the men for Confederate service. Montgomery, Tennessee, was the area chosen for the new recruiting station.

Montgomery was two miles from the Louisville and Nashville railroad and seven miles from Clarksville in a heavy timbered forest, well supplied with water, while fields furnished sufficient open space for drilling large commands. In July 1861, Camp Boone was laid out and cleared of undergrowth. Young men rallied from all parts of Kentucky and from places as far away as Indiana to join the new command. The first Confederate Kentucky unit to arrive at Camp Boone was the Second Kentucky Volunteer Infantry commanded by Colonel Roger Hanson. The men immediately started to set up their tents and the officers began training the men in the fine art of drill and military discipline.

Colonels Lloyd Tilghman and R. P. Trabue were also given permission to raise a regiment. Colonel Tilghman was a commander in the Kentucky State Guard in Paducah, Kentucky, and was asked by Confederate General Simon Bolivar Buckner if he would command the Third Kentucky. His unit arrived into Camp Boone shortly after Wither's unit. The Second Kentucky Infantry was officially organized on July 17, 1861. The Third Kentucky was organized a couple of days later. The officers that made up the Third Kentucky were Colonel Lloyd Tilghman, Lt. Colonel Albert Thompson, Major Ben Anderson, Captain Albert Boyd, Captain J. S. Byers, Dr. J. W. Thompson, and Dr. J. B. Sanders. Colonel Tilghman was promoted to Brigadier General in the fall and would later be sent to command Fort Henry and Donelson. Since Tilghman was an engineer, the Confederate government thought that Tilghman's skills would be put to better use in the construction of these two forts. The Third Kentucky, although not officially part of the First Kentucky Brigade, fought with Breckinridge[1a].

Early in August, a battery of six brass cannon, cast at Memphis, under Captain Ed P. Byrne, arrived at Camp Boone. Confederate Governor of Kentucky George W. Johnson came and enlisted as a private in the Confederate army. Unfortunately he would later be killed at the Battle of Shiloh in April 1862.

About the same time, the first companies or parts of companies, designed for Colonel Robert Trabue's regiment, came out and prepared Camp Burnett, three miles south of Boone. The companies were rapidly filled up and the Fourth Kentucky was organized in September.

Other units that were organized were the Sixth Kentucky commanded by Colonel Joseph Lewis and the Ninth Kentucky commanded by Colonel Thomas Hunt. The Kentucky Brigade was four thousand men strong, filled with pride, and determined to set their state free from what they perceived as Union domination.

The first formal announcement of the Brigade was on October 28, 1861, when Confederate General Albert Sidney Johnston, who commanded the Western District, gave General Order No. 51. The brigade was commanded by Brigadier General's Simon Bolivar Buckner, John C. Breckinridge, William Preston, Roger Hanson, Ben Hardin Helm, and Joseph Lewis.

In 1861 Union General Ulysses Grant entered Paducah and forced the 3rd Kentucky to Camp Burnett, in Bowling Green, Kentucky, along with the rest of the 1st Kentucky Brigade. By February of 1862, the 1st Kentucky Brigade was forced to train at Camp Boone, in Tennessee. Arming the 1st Kentucky Brigade was difficult. The guns supplied to the Kentucky Brigade were the old flintlock muskets Models 1808-1822, .69 caliber Belgian muskets and sometimes the Kentucky long rifle. Soldiers didn't like the old muskets because they had a tendency to burst. Many Confederate soldiers had no weapons at all in 1861.

The lack of clothing was also a problem. In 1861, the 1st Kentucky Brigade wore pretty much what they brought with them. Colonel Lloyd Tilghman, commander of the 3rd Kentucky Infantry in 1861, wrote constantly to Albert Sidney Johnston for uniforms and weapons but to no avail. Lloyd Tilghman mentions in one of his reports that some of the uniforms were being made by several ladies. Just prior to and after the Battle of Shiloh in April of 1862, the 1st Kentucky Brigade managed to re-arm itself with the .577 caliber British Enfield rifles. Uniforms were also shipped to the 1st Kentucky Brigade by the different government supply depots.

After the Battle of Perryville, in October of 1862, Kentucky would remain in Union control. Because of this, the 1st Kentucky Brigade would be in exile and never saw their home state again until the war ended.

The 1st Kentucky Brigade became part of the Army of the Tennessee and was known as a hard fighting unit. The Brigade participated in the battles of Shiloh, Corinth, Vicksburg, Baton Rouge, Stone's River, Jackson, Chickamauga, and Missionary Ridge, as well as throughout the Atlanta campaign and against Sherman during his march to the sea. During the final months of the war, the 1st Kentucky Brigade became mounted and served in the eastern theater. The last of the 1st Kentucky Brigade surrendered on May 1865, at Washington, Georgia. Because the 1st Kentucky Brigade was not allowed to recruit from its home state after 1862, the numbers of the Orphan Brigade dwindled quickly. Only five hundred of the original four thousand members of the brigade remained when they surrendered in 1865.

During the battle of Stone's River from December 31st, 1862, to January 2nd, 1863, Confederate Division commander of the 1st Confederate Brigade, General John C. Breckinridge coined the famous phrase "the Orphan Brigade" when he lost four hundred men out of his 1,200 in the fatal charge on the last day of battle.

Breckinridge rode among the survivors crying, "My poor orphans! My poor orphans!" During that same battle, the 1st Kentucky Brigade would lose General Roger Hanson. Another famous Confederate General of the 1st Kentucky Brigade, Ben Hardin Helm – who was Lincoln's brother in law – was killed at the Battle of Chickamauga on September 1863.

Confederate General John C. Breckinridge, commander of the Orphan Brigade, or the Kentucky Confederate troops. *Courtesy Library of Congress.*

Little did these men of Boone know what awaited them on the bloody battlefields of Shiloh, Stone's River, and Chickamauga. Many a comrade fell upon soil that they had never seen before. They died in places the men had never seen or heard of before they joined the Orphan Brigade. The reason Camp Boone may be so haunted is for the sheer fact that while there many of the men were still filled with pride and joy, with patriotism and a sense of duty to their State. These were the happiest times for these men. Many likely thought they did not want to miss out on the fight to come. Some of these men formed strong friendships while at Camp Boone, only later to lose their good friends in the killing fields. The soldiers seem to return to experience those happy times again.

The Ghost of Colonel Roger Hanson

Many years ago the Third Kentucky Infantry re-enactment group camped at Camp Boone They drilled and organized for the New Year's battle engagements. It was during one these encampments when a re-enactor got the experience of his life.

While walking in one of the many large fields where the original Kentucky units drilled in 1861, one of the members of the Third Kentucky re-enactors heard talking behind him. He quickly turned around and to his amazement Col. Roger Hanson was standing before him.

There is no mistaking Col. Hanson. He was a very large, heavy set man, with a goatee. Roger Hanson was born on August 27th, 1827, and was raised in Winchester, Kentucky. Hanson had an illustrious career even before he joined the Orphan Brigade. He served as a Lieutenant in the Mexican War, was a lawyer and was a state legislator for Kentucky in 1853 and 1855. Just before the Civil War broke out, Roger Hanson was a colonel of the Kentucky State Guard. At the Battle of Stone's River Hanson was mortally wounded. He died on January 4th, 1863. But yet here he was in all his glory.

The re-enactor was shocked at first but then became intrigued at what Roger Hanson was doing. It seems that Roger Hanson was upset at what the soldier was wearing. He was barking orders at the re-enactor at his dress and was directing him to shape up. It seems that Roger Hanson was reliving his old times when he had his hands full with new recruits. Many of these young boys didn't have a clue on how to march, use a weapon or even how to maintain a neat appearance.

The Confederate re-enactor just stood in amazement as Roger Hanson gave orders to him. The conversation lasted for about a half hour. As soon as Roger Hanson was through with his orders, he disappeared as quickly as he had appeared. It is interesting to note that the Confederate re-enactor tried to talk to Col. Roger Hanson but the ghost just seemed to be talking to another, unseen soldier. Every time Roger Hanson spoke there would be some silence as if another person was speaking. Then Roger Hanson again began to speak. Maybe spirits are like broken records and play out their parts over and over again. It may be a glitch in time in which the soldier is doomed to repeat his actions.

Kentucky native Colonel Roger Hanson, who was killed at the Battle of Stone's River, Tennessee. His ghost has been seen commanding his troops one last time at Camp Boone, Tennessee. *Courtesy Library of Congress.*

The Ghost with a Sense of Humor

A group of Confederate re-enactors walked in one of the large fields at Camp Boone at night. They took their candle burning lanterns. It was a cold moonlit night and snow from a recent snowstorm covered the ground. On the back side of the field is a large wooded area where a wagon trail once went through. Once past the field the wooded area opens up into another field. The re-enactors came near one of the wooded areas when one of the male members of the group took out a flask of whiskey from his frock coat. The re-enactor asked if anyone would like a sip of his elixir.

From the woods came a voice of a boy, possibly in his teens, who said "Yeah, sure I'll take a sip."

The whole group turned to the woods to see who was talking to them. No one was found.

The re-enactors turned around and started to return to their tents when the re-enactor yelled to the woods "You are too young to drink!"

All of the sudden out of the woods came a snow ball which hit the re-enactor square in the back of the head.

The re-enactor quickly whipped around and headed for the woods but no one was found.

Love Beyond the Grave

A most disturbing story comes from a female re-enactor who went into the field and was walking along when a ghostly apparition approached her. It was a man in his thirties who approached the female re-enactor. The man told the woman that he was going to die soon and would she please deliver his wedding ring to his wife. The Confederate ghost pulled off his ring and tried to give it to the female re-enactor.

The ring was placed in her hand and the woman promised to return the ring to his wife. She asked what his name was. He responded and told her. After the incident occurred the female re-enactor tried to find the ring and tell others of her experience. She searched everywhere but no ring was to be found.

Later, when the female re-enactor returned home, she looked up the Confederate soldier's name. To her amazement, he really existed and was killed at the Battle of Stone's River.

In this encounter it might appear that a soldier shared a premonition of his death and displayed his devotion to his wife. In real life history one wonders if the soldier indeed was able to return the wedding ring to his wife or did he die leaving his final wish unfulfilled.

A Father Looks for His Son

A sad tale from Camp Boone tells of an incident that occurred in many households in Kentucky. Since Kentucky declared its neutrality in 1861, the male members of the household decided on which side they wanted to fight. This policy literally divided families.

There were many instances of father against son, brother against brother. One of the more famous familial divisions was that of Kentucky Senator John Crittenden who had two sons who fought for both sides. Thomas Crittenden served as a General for the Union army and his brother George Crittenden fought as a General for the Confederate army. Kentucky Senator Henry Clay, the Great Compromiser, had three grandsons who fought for the Confederate side and four grandsons who fought for the Union side. Col. Roger Hanson had a brother, Charles Hanson, who was a Union soldier. President Abraham Lincoln's brother in law was Confederate General Ben Hardin Helm, who was killed at the Battle of Chickamauga. When Lincoln learned of Helm's death, the news threw the entire White House into mourning. Lincoln had tried to persuade Helm to take a position in the Union army but it was of no use.

In many a household in Kentucky, a son chose a side with which the father didn't agree. Words were spoken in haste and the son stomped out the house to join the cause he felt was right. The father yelled back in anger and told his son that he is no longer wanted in the house as long he joins that army. Later both sides regretted what they had said to each other but it was then too late. The son had joined the army and was unable to leave his unit and return home.

Along one of the old campgrounds at Camp Boone there is a wooded edge along a field. The sound of a large thud is heard as if a body hit the ground and then someone gasps. Many believe that the body is that of an older man.

The story goes that a son left his home to join the Confederate army. The father tried to persuade his son to stay home but the son did not listen. He stormed out of the door to join the Confederates at Camp Boone. One night the son was put on picket duty to protect the camp. Across the field, an older man came at him.

The new soldier yelled out, "Halt, Who goes there!"

The soldier's heart raced with thoughts and images of an impending attack.

Again the soldier cried out, "Halt, Who goes there!"

The figure continued to approach the young soldier. In the excitement, the soldier fired his weapon. The older man fell upon the ground with a heavy thud. A gasp arose and then all was quiet. The camp was immediately awakened by the sound and soldiers came scrambling out of their tents. The officers formed the men, expecting an attack. The officer of the day came to the young boy with a lamp to see what all the commotion was about. The boy told him that he had shot an intruder in camp. The officer walked to the lifeless body and put his lantern light upon it. In the shock and horror, the son realized he shot his own father!

One wonders if the sound of the falling body is indeed the same father's death spoken of in folklore. Is this spectral sound an oft-repeated sign of punishment for the poor young lad who shot his own father?

The Confederate Surgeon

During one summer's encampment, a Confederate surgeon was invited to participate in the drills and activities. As the moon shone bright, the Confederate surgeon re-enactor walked in the field with several others.

The Confederate re-enactor walked toward the wagon trail along the wooded area of the field. The other re-enactors then noticed that the Confederate surgeon was immobile as if in complete shock.

They tried to move him but he would not budge. All that was apparent on his face was a countenance of complete horror. They finally yelled at him and the mysterious and terrifying hold upon him broke. He ran from the field and quickly made it back to the camping area and his tent. The other re-enactors quickly chased behind him.

When they caught up with him, they asked what he had seen. The Confederate surgeon was still pale and shaking from his experience. He said that he was looking into a small ravine near the wooded edge of the field when to his horror he saw a Confederate soldier upon the ground with a large gaping hole in the chest. The body was covered in a pool of blood.

This amazed the other re-enactors, they had seen nothing in the same area. Only the petrified Confederate re-enactor had seen this horrible sight. Was the Confederate surgeon re-enactor more sympathetic to the battlefield atrocities? Perhaps the ghost of the wounded soldier thought the surgeon could help him?

Whatever the reason for this unexplained encounter, the shocked re-enactor was not prepared for this grisly sight. Although re-enactors think they understand the combat experience, they really have no clue what the poor soldier during the Civil War went through. We can only imagine the damage done by soft lead bullets from weapons of calibers of .54 to .75 or the force ripping away flesh and bone. The artillery upon the battlefield fired canister shot and shell at soldiers with ranges of only 200 to 600 yards, unleashing a horror of hundreds of small iron balls hurling themselves through the heads and intestines of soldiers without armor. The gore and smell of a battlefield can only be imagined. If we did see such an incident, maybe our reaction would be the same as the Confederate surgeon's.

Phantom Sounds of Battle

Another Confederate re-enactor also tells of his experience in the field. This re-enactor walked the same field and heard horses at a full gallop ride across the field, although there were no horses visible. A thud was heard in a corner of the field. And voices of men laughing and marching across the wagon trail were heard although there was no one of the road.

In the days of the Civil War, many of the soldiers did picket duty on the wagon trail to make sure no foe was approaching. It is good to hear voices of laughter ring upon the air. Perhaps these soldiers still enjoy talks by campfire, stories of home, tales of how it was to drill for the first time, or their first experiences of marching in step or cautionary stories of dealing with their officers.

The Soldier
Evading the Army

One of the officers of the Third Kentucky Infantry re-enactment group talks about the group performing a tactical exercise in the woods and fields around Camp Boone. A tactical is when two units are put upon the field and each side does not know each other's location. The goal is to capture the soldiers from the other side.

During one of the tactical exercises, one of the officers saw a Confederate soldier quickly run into a barn. The officer wanted to capture the lone soldier. He decided to flank the barn so that the soldier could not escape. The unit was broken into two sections. One half headed for the front of the barn and the other went around back. The two units arrived at the barn and charged in from both ends. To their shock and embarrassment, no one was in the barn. When the soldiers returned to camp after the tactical, they asked all around for the soldier that they saw enter the barn. No one in the unit fit the description of the mystery soldier.

The Battle of Shiloh, Tennessee

One of the most haunted battlefields in the Western Theater, other than Perryville, must be Shiloh. After the battle of Shiloh, it was said that the South would never smile again. Thousands of men lost their lives during the battle. Places such as the Hornet's Nest and the Bloody Pond would become some of the most hotly contested locations on the battlefield. The battle occurred in April of 1862.

After the fall of Forts Henry and Donelson in February of 1862, Union General Ulysses S. Grant was free to move into Tennessee. Grant arrived at Pittsburgh Landing in March of 1862. Union General Henry Halleck, Commander of all forces in the West, ordered General Don Carlos

Officers of the 114th Pennsylvania Infantry, August 1864. *Courtesy of the Library of Congress.*

Buell's army at Nashville to join Grant at Pittsburg Landing and then to attack Corinth, Mississippi. Confederate General Albert Sidney Johnston concentrated his forces at Corinth to oppose Grant. By the end of March, he had 44,000 men, commanded by Lt. Gen. Leonidas Polk, Maj. Gen. John Breckinridge, Gen. Braxton Bragg, and Major General William Hardee.

They would be facing Ulysses Grant's 39,000 men. Johnston knew that he must attack Grant before Buell's 36,000 men reached Pittsburg Landing. Grant was not expecting an attack, so no defensive plans were formulated and no trenches or earthworks were dug. Sherman set up his headquarters at a place called Shiloh church. Since Grant assumed that there would be no attack, he placed Sherman's raw recruits in the advance position. Because of rain and a lost division under Bragg, Johnston was not able to reach Pittsburg Landing until April 6th.[1]

Johnston's troops were then less than two miles from the Federal camps. At 5:00 A.M. on Sunday morning, April 6, 1862, Union Major James Powell of the 25th Missouri and 300 men scouted the area and collided with Confederate Major Aaron Hardcastle's 3rd Mississippi Infantry Battalion, the advance guard of Wood's brigade, Hardee's Corps.

The Confederates fired and the Federals under Powell stood their ground as reinforcements were brought up. Jesse Appler of the 53rd Ohio deployed his men but soon fell back before the massive Confederate onslaught. Cleburne now began to advance, his goal being to seize the crossroads at Shiloh church. Braxton Bragg moved up to support William Hardee. Grant then called for Buell's troops who arrived in Savannah the day before and were on the east bank of the river.

Grant also called for Lew Wallace to get his men ready to move out. At 9:00 A.M. Grant rode from his headquarters to the front. By 10:00 A.M., the Confederates had driven through the camps of three Union divisions, sending the surprised blue-clad soldiers reeling back toward the river. Union General Benjamin M. Prentiss's division was pushed back almost a mile. The Confederates stopped at Prentiss' camp and began to eat the food that Prestiss' men were cooking for their breakfast.

This gave Prentiss time to take up a good defensive position on high ground along a sunken road. About 1,000 men formed along the road, which was about a mile behind their original position. Other units formed on either side of Prentiss. Hurlbut sent two brigades on his left and W.H. L. Wallace aligned three brigades on Prentiss flanks, two on Prentiss right and one to his far left, beyond Hurlbut. To the right of Wallace were two

Confederate troops rout Union soldier from their camps, Battle of Shiloh, Tennessee. *Courtesy of the Library of Congress.*

brigades of McClernand's division and Sherman's division. These troops made a desperate attempt to slow the Confederate advance. Union Gen. Ulysses Grant looked over the new line and ordered Prentiss to "maintain that position at all hazards."[2]

Cheatham's division advanced upon the new Federal line and when they came within 150 yards, the Federals unleashed their artillery. At 30 yards, Union Col. William Shaw and his 14th Iowa fired at the oncoming Confederates. The Confederate line fell back. On Cheatham's extreme right, Union Brig. Gen. Jacob Lauman's brigade of Hurlbut's division took on the Confederates. His men opened fire on the Rebels at 100 yards but the Confederates approached until they were within ten yards of the 31st Indiana before they were stopped.[3]

The Rebel troops under Braxton Bragg continued crashing and screaming through the woods, toward the Federal position. Bragg ordered the 4th, 13th, and the 19th Louisiana and the 1st Arkansas to attack the Federals on the sunken road. Charge after charge—twelve in all—was made against Prentiss's position and each was repulsed with great slaughter.[4]

"It's a hornet's nest in there!" cried the Rebels, recoiling from the blasts of canister and case shot and the fire from the 8th Iowa's eight hundred rifles.

By 2:30 P.M., after two hours of fighting, the Confederates were no closer to taking the Federal lines at the Hornet's Nest than they were at the Sunken Road. The Confederate onslaught began to grind to a halt.[5]

There were massive problems on the field. There was no overall Confederate commander and no coherent plan of attack. The Confederates had 17,000 men against Grant's 4,000 men under Prentiss but the Confederate troops were sent in piecemeal. Orders were given and then countermanded by different generals. At some points along the line, Confederate companies halted because there were no further orders for them. Beauregard was in the rear and did not know what was going on at the front and only sent men to where he heard fighting. Corps commanders reduced themselves to small unit commanders.[6]

A Confederate attack led by General Albert Sidney Johnston broke through Union troops in the Peach Orchard on Prentiss's left, led by the Kentucky troops under Gen. John C. Breckinridge. The Rebels pushed back the troops on his right, leaving what was left of Prentiss's division without support. Johnston led the Kentucky Confederate troops toward the Peach Orchard but about half way there he was struck in the leg by a bullet that severed a major artery. The blood flowed into his boot. Johnston soon became disoriented and dismounted. He had a field tourniquet in his pocket but his officers didn't know how to use it and earlier in the battle he sent his personal surgeon, Dr. Yandell, away to tend to the wounded soldiers. General Johnston soon bled to death.[7]

Union General Prentiss on horseback seen directing the Union defense of the Hornet's Nest, Battle of Shiloh, Tennessee. *Courtesy of the Library of Congress.*

The Peach Orchard at the Shiloh Battlefield, Tennessee.

After Albert Sidney Johnston's death, General P.G.T. Beauregard took command of the Rebel forces. Beauregard now was obsessed with the Hornet's Nest. He could have gone to the flanks and driven the Federals right into the river at Pittsburg Landing, but he chose not to.[8]

Beauregard soon massed the largest assembly of cannon in the War up to that point, sixty-two in all, and he aimed them at point blank range at the Hornet's Nest and the Sunken Road. At about 4:00 P.M. he began a bombardment with shell and canister that was like "a mighty hurricane sweeping everything before it." The Hornet's Nest exploded under the fire but still Prentiss and his men held on, their lines bending back into a horseshoe shape as more and more pressure was applied to their flanks. By 5:30 they were completely surrounded and being attacked on all sides.[9]

Unable to do any more to obey Grant's order to hold his position, Prentiss ordered a cease-fire and surrendered his remaining 2,200 men at 6:00 P.M.. However, his gallant defense had given Grant the time he needed to construct a new line to the rear. Grant's new line ran inland at a right angle from the river above Pittsburgh Landing northwest toward Owl Creek. The line was three miles long and strongly defended. Col. J.D. Webster grouped cannon on the left of the line while Sherman and McClernand protected a road that ran north parallel to the Tennessee River. Lew Wallace arrived at 7:00 P.M. and set up at the far right of the new line. Col. Jacob Ammen's brigade from Buell's corps arrived. The division commander, Brig. Gen. William Nelson and his men followed Ammen's brigade across the river and took their positions on Grant's new line.[10]

The Confederates were fighting for twelve hours and were exhausted and hungry, having not eaten since 3:00 A.M. that morning. Many of the Confederates refused to go on and sat down in the abandoned Federal camps and began to eat. Most of the Confederates believed they had won a great victory and thought they had beaten most of the Union forces. Bragg and Polk tried to rally the men for one more attack before darkness set in. Bragg, on the left, could only gather Chalmers's troops and John Jackson's men, who were already out of ammunition. Bragg's two divisions tried to rush the new line but Federal artillery ripped Bragg's men to pieces. Polk and Hardee, on the right, fought with Sherman's and McClernand's troops but were not successful in capturing any of them. As twilight settled Beauregard suspended the assault on the Federals, and recalled Polk and Bragg.[11]

During the night, Nathan Bedford Forrest's cavalry scouted the Federal lines. Forrest reported to Hardee that Grant now had about 45,000 men against their 20,000 Confederates. Grant decided that he would attack the Confederates the next day.[12]

On April 7, 1862, the Union forces rolled forward at about 7:30 A.M. and the outnumbered Confederates were pushed back. Grant took back most of the ground he had lost the previous day. Cleburne put up some resistance around Shiloh Church, leading an attack on Sherman's men but his soldiers became entangled in the thick undergrowth and soon his lines were decimated by the Federals. Confederate Brig. Gen. Sterling A. M. Wood tried to hold Shiloh Church, but his left was crumbling and as his flanks became exposed to Federal fire, he pulled back.[13]

At 2:30 P.M., Beauregard ordered a withdrawal to Corinth.

An hour later, the Confederates began to withdraw. The Union troops were just as exhausted as the Confederates and did not pursue them. On April 8th, Nathan Bedford Forrest's cavalry troops, the rear guard for the Confederates, were overtaken by Sherman's skirmishers. Forrest led a charge against them but outdistanced his men in the process and soon realized that he was alone against 2,000 Federals, all aiming their rifles at him. Forrest was shot in the side by a Federal soldier. The bullet lodged against Forrest's spine but somehow he managed to pick up a Federal soldier and use him as a shield and ride back to his own lines.[14]

Forrest was the last man to be injured in the Battle of Shiloh, the first great bloody battle of the war. Union losses were 13,047. Confederate losses were 10,694. Halleck arrived at Pittsburgh Landing on April 11th and removed Grant from field command. Halleck personally organized the army into a 100,000 man force with 200 cannon and arrived on the outskirts of Corinth on May 28th. Beauregard, outnumbered two to one, tried to trick Halleck into thinking that Confederates had more men by sending trains in and out of Corinth.[15]

With each arriving train the townspeople and soldiers gave a great cheer as if a new train load of soldiers arrived. The ruse worked well and bought Beauregard enough time to safely escort his men out of town. On May 30th, the Federals entered a deserted Corinth and seized the Memphis & Charleston railroad.[16]

Confederate President Jefferson Davis said, "This railroad was the vertebra of the West" and now it was in Federal hands. The Battle of Shiloh will go down as the ninth most costly battle of the Civil War.

The Ghosts in the Hornets Nest

On many a cold night re-enactors heard screams and moans coming from the Hornet's Nest. Many people have claimed that the area of the Hornet's Nest is extremely difficult to photograph. Either their camera locks up when they try to take the photograph or the film does not develop. Many believe that the moans and cries heard by tourists and re-enactors are the same sounds from the soldiers who lived through or died in the horror of the Hornet's nest.

Arkansas monument located at the Hornet's Nest, Battle of Shiloh, Tennessee.
[Photograph from an early 1930's Shiloh National Battlefield postcard from Bryan Bush's personal collection.]

The Cavalrymen

One re-enactor told me a story about cavalrymen wandering the fields of Shiloh. This happened during one of the National Events. These are when thousands of re-enactors gather together to re-enact battles. A Confederate cavalryman was posted to protect the camps at night. With these large gatherings of people, it is easy for unscrupulous people to steal valuable items. This particular Confederate Cavalryman re-enactor was told to patrol the sutler's area. Sutler's areas are set up in authentic tents selling many items that the typical re-enactor needs such as black powder, percussion caps, uniforms, etc. and is not much different than what would have happened during the Civil War. Many of the officers during the Civil War did not like the sutlers because they sometimes provided alcohol to the men or sold items such as pies and cakes with expensive price tags.

While the Confederate cavalry re-enactor was riding sutler's row at night, he noticed several other Confederate cavalrymen approaching on the other side of the sutler's row. Curious as to why these men rode around at night and so close to sutler's row, he decided to check them out and say, "Hi." As he rode toward the Confederate cavalrymen, they started to ride away.

The re-enactor quickly jabbed at his horse's side to make the beast ride faster. The re-enactor was now chasing after the Confederate cavalrymen at a breakneck speed to catch up with them. All of the sudden the Confederate riders disappeared into the fog, leaving the Confederate re-enactor stunned and confused. He did not speak of his experience to anyone until confiding in me...

The Bloody Pond

During the battle of Shiloh, many of the wounded men crawled past the Peach Orchard and headed for a small pond that was the only source of water. Confederate and Union alike were drinking from the pond. Many of the men took their last drink from the pond before dying. Others bled into the pond, making the entire pond turn a dark red from all the blood.

While the author was working as a tour guide for a Civil War museum in Bardstown, Kentucky, one of the displays in the museum was on Shiloh. After the tour the museum, visitors would relay their stories about visiting the Bloody Pond. Several of the visitors to the battlefield told the same story. Four separate times tourists relayed the same story.

When the visitor got out of his or her car and walked toward the Bloody Pond, the visitor would immediately break out in a sweat and become sick to the stomach. The pain intensified as the individual got closer to the Bloody Pond. Before long, each returned to their cars fearing that they would throw up or pass out. Their spouses immediately became alarmed at seeing the sickness in their loved ones' faces.

The Bloody Pond located at the Shiloh National Park. During the battle, wounded soldiers crawled to the pond for water; by the end of the battle, the pond was filled with human blood. The ghost of a Confederate soldier has been seen at the Bloody Pond and many visitors claim to become violently ill when they approach the pond.

As soon as the afflicted tourists headed back into their cars, the nausea quickly faded, leaving them sweat-soaked and confused. One wonders what repeatedly caused this illness in the visitors to the Bloody Pond. Perhaps tourists were forced to experience the desperate illness which the wounded soldiers had as they headed toward the pond for their last drink.

In addition, many tourists claimed that when they kicked the dirt around the Bloody Pond, the ground begins to ooze blood. Could this simply be the red clay mixing with water to produce a quality similar to blood? Or is the bloody soil a lingering psychic effect from the blood of wounded soldiers?

Shiloh Church

During the Battle of Shiloh, Sherman's men were pushed back by the onslaught of Confederate troops. Some of Sherman's artifacts were even captured by the Confederates. One story comes from a fellow re-enactor who visited the Church on a quiet Sunday afternoon.

To his amazement, while he was looking at some of the graves that are located near the church, he began to hear the faint sound of wagon wheels hitting the ground and the sounds of chains clanking. The sound

On April 6, 1862, Union General William T. Sherman held the area around Shiloh Church, but during the battle he was forced to fall back and Confederate General P. G. T. Beauregard made the Shiloh Church his headquarters. Ghostly sounds of wagons have been heard coming from the site. *[Photograph from an early 1930's Shiloh National Battlefield postcard from Bryan Bush's personal collection.]*

began to get louder. He did not think it was too out of the ordinary, since another re-enacting group was in the area and pulled a wagon. He turned around to see the wagon heading down the road but there was no vehicle to be seen and the sound stopped. Even though the battle of Shiloh was over a hundred years past, the sound of men moving wagons and soldiers on the move remains to speak to our imagination.

The Battle of Franklin, Tennessee

On November 22, 1864, Confederate General John Bell Hood's 39,000 Confederates left Florence, Alabama, in three columns commanded by Maj. Gen. Benjamin Cheatham, Lt. Generals Stephen D. Lee and Alexander Stewart. Following a plan originated by Hood and approved by Jefferson Davis, they invaded Tennessee to draw Union military attention from the Deep South, to crush Maj. Gen. William T. Sherman's Western support for his operations in Georgia, and perhaps take the war through Kentucky to the North.[1]

After the fall of Atlanta, Hood moved the Army of Tennessee northwest in September and October, drawing Sherman and a detached force from Atlanta, skirmishing and wrecking railroads, fighting at Alatoona, and then withdrawing into northwest Alabama. Sherman had followed them west of Rome, Georgia, and unwilling to pursue farther, ordered the IV, XVI, and XXIII Corps to Major General George Thomas, at Nashville and returned to Atlanta to begin his March to the Sea. Sherman knew Hood's intent and believed that if reinforced, Thomas would repel him.[2]

Hood and Thomas spent more than twenty days preparing for their parts in the campaign. Hood gathered supplies, reorganized and waited for Major General Nathan Forrest's cavalry. Thomas created a cavalry force under Brigadier General James Wilson and moved the IV and XXIII Corps from the Chattanooga area to positions west along the Tennessee and Alabama Railroad. The XVI Corps detachment Thomas awaited could not reach him until December. Forrest spent late October and early November raiding Nashville, Tennessee's supply lines and wrecking the railroad at Johnsonville.[3]

Forrest joined Hood at Florence, the expedition entered Tennessee, and its columns traveling miles apart, moved for Columbia, halfway to Nashville. The XXIII Corps, under Maj. Gen. John Schofield and elements of the IV Corps were at Pulaski along the railroad, west of the invading columns. On George Thomas' orders, Schofield raced his force north to Columbia, arriving ahead of the Confederates on November 24th and covered the bridges over the Duck River astride the invasion route. Federal cavalry sparred with Confederate horsemen from the Alabama line to Columbia. Schofield skirmished around Columbia from the 24th to the 26th until Hood's columns converged on his front. Bridges over the Duck River were destroyed and Schofield's troops withdrew north, covering the fords until Forrest's cavalry crossed at Henry's Mill, on Schofield's left, on the 28th.[4]

Wilson sent word to Schofield, "Get back to Franklin without delay."

Union Major General David Stanley, commanding IV Corps troops, hurried north to Spring Hill November 29 to hold the town until Schofield's troops passed through. Forrest, with his eastern crossing of the Duck River, threatened the Federal right. Stanley's pickets held him off. Hood failed in his plan to hold the Federals, circumvent them, and press on to Nashville. He blamed Cheatham for bungled enveloping maneuvers as Schofield slipped through, marching his men from midnight to noon from Spring Hill to Franklin, on November 30th.[5]

When Hood found out that Schoefield and his Federals had escaped, he blamed Cheatham. He called all of his officers a bunch of cowards and said the only way to cure a coward is to throw him into battle.

Schofield was now at Franklin and he began to dig trenches and rifle pits. He deployed two divisions of the XXIII Corps to dig in astride the turnpike and then deployed one division from the IV Corps on the right flank. The headquarters were set up at the Fountain Branch Carter House, which stood on the high point of a wide plain almost devoid of trees. If Hood planned to attack, it would be over two miles of open ground starting from a low ridge to the south known as Winstead Hill. Schofield set up his dozen guns on the far side of the Harpeth River, at a place called Fort Granger.[6]

Hood reached Franklin at 2 P.M. and sent Stewart's Corps forward to flank the hill and force the Federals off of it, then rode up and took a look at the Federal army. Against the advice of his generals, Hood decided to order a frontal attack on the Union position without artillery support. Hood was going to send Cheatham's and Stewart's divisions directly at the middle of the Union trenches. He thought that this would teach Cheatham's men a lesson by not allowing Union General Schofield's men to escape again as he had done on November 30, 1864, and making sure Cheatham's men were fighting men and not cowards. He would send the units in one at a time, instead of en masse, and would only send seven of his eighteen brigades at the Union position.

The seven brigades belonged to General's John Brown's and Patrick Cleburne's Divisions. Brown put two brigades under Generals States Rights Gist and George Washington Gordon who made up the front line. Two other brigades under Brig. Gen. John Carter and Otho Strahl formed the second line. From Cleburne's Division, General Hiram Granbury's Texas brigade was on the left and Daniel Govan's brigade was in the center. Mark Lowrey's brigade formed the right.[7]

The other division in Cheatham's Corps consisted of the three brigades in Bate's Division. General Bate's brigades were on the left flank, and were to make an attack in conjunction with a division of Forrest's cavalry. On the far right flank, Loring's and Walthall's Divisions, in Stewart's Corps, were deployed with their right flank on the Harpeth River. Forrest and two of his divisions would try and drive back the Federal cavalry under General Wilson who was north of the river.[8]

The Federals dug two sets of trenches to cover the gap left between the Columbia Turnpike and the breastworks. On both sides of the turnpike, the main line angled back in gradual steps conforming to the perimeter of the town of Franklin. A second line protecting the turnpike angled back similarly on higher ground. Here more artillery was deployed to fire over the first line and sweep the field in front. The Confederates would attack the most vulnerable Yankee position.

George Wagner's division, acting as the Federal rear guard, was pushed into the trenches by Stewart's flanking movement and abandoned Winstead Hill. Wagner formed a reserve near the Carter house. Wagner thought that he was supposed to hold where he was, no matter what happened to his exposed forward position. A half hour before sunset, Hood advanced. The Confederates charged Wagner's position and Wagner's Yankee's ran for the safety of the Federal lines. The Union artillery and rifleman in the Federal works were not able to fire upon the advancing Confederates because Wagner's retreating men got in their way and they were afraid that they would shoot their own men. The Confederates charged into the first works. The 104th Ohio panicked and ran and that led to other units running. The guns on either side of the pike and the works on the east and west of the pike were abandoned and Cleburne and Brown's men took possession of the recently vacated works.

Union Colonel Opdycke's men were posted two hundred yards behind the Carter House. When they heard the firing on the works, they rushed forward with reinforcements, two Kentucky regiments and the remnant of Wagner's other two brigades. Hand to hand fighting broke out between the Confederates and Yankees. Hood had no reserves to back up the initial assault and the Confederates began to fall back inside the Federal trench line, then over the earthworks to huddle on the other side.

Federal troops reoccupied the main line and threw up a barricade that plugged the gap. The assault by Stewart's men on the Federal left was going well until they reached a railroad cut where Federal artillery from across the Harpeth River to the east, pounded their position. The Confederates got entangled in a grove of locust trees that the Federals had turned into an abatis. (An abatis is a defensive obstacle made by laying felled trees on top of each other with branches, sometimes sharpened, facing the enemy.) The Henry repeating rifles from Colonel John Casement's brigade ripped large holes in the Confederate lines and stopped them in their tracks.

One of Walthall's brigades, led by Brigadier General William Quarles, broke through the Federal earthworks, only to be pinned down by crossfire. Quarles was hit in the head. Artillery fire also decimated Maj. Gen. William Loring's Division, which was advancing on the far right. Other Confederate casualties included Brig. Gen. John Adams, who was shot when he tried to take the earthworks. He urged his men forward and led them directly into the Federal earthwork, and even tried to take the colors of the 65th Illinois. Adams later died of his wounds.

Farther to the right, Loring's other brigades under Brig. Gen. Winfield Featherston fell back. Loring himself rode out in front of his men and headed for the Federal earthworks. He tried to break the Yankee line but he was pinned down by the Federal fire. Both Loring and Walthall were within a few hundred yards of the works but they were both stalemated and could advance no farther.

The Confederate left also stalled. General Bate got close enough to order an attack on the works but darkness set in and his force was small. The defenders, two divisions under Gen. Nathan Kimball and Thomas Ruger, kept the Confederates from advancing any farther.

The Yankees couldn't escape until the bridges over the Harpeth River were repaired. Now the Yankees and Confederates were separated by only a hundred yards in some areas and in other areas only by a few feet. The attack cost the lives of General Dams, Brig. Gen. Hiram Granbury, General States Rights Gist, General Patrick Cleburne, and General Strahl. General Gordon surrendered, Col. F.E.P. Stafford was killed, and Maj. General John Brown wounded.

Hood also lost 7,000 men, 1,750 killed and the rest were wounded or taken prisoner. The Federals lost 1,222 killed and wounded, and 1,104 missing and presumed taken prisoner, mostly from Wagner's division. Schofield ordered a retreat and tried to repair the bridges across the Harpeth River at their backs. The Union retreat, stalled by the destroyed bridges, began again at 11 P.M. and continued toward Thomas's Nashville lines the next day. At Franklin, Hood's last attempt to keep the IV and XXIII corps from reaching George Thomas at Nashville failed.

Hood woke up in the morning and saw that Schofield's men had evacuated Franklin and decided to pursue them and by 1 P.M., Hood's men were traveling north after Schofield, thinking that they had won a great victory.

Schofield reached Nashville on December 1st. Three divisions, 13,000 men strong, of the XVI corps, under Maj. Gen. Andrew Smith reached Nashville on November 30, from the Trans-Mississippi. Schofield's arrival brought Thomas' strength to nearly 70,000. Hood arrived at the outskirts of Nashville on December 1st. At this point, Hood had only 30,000 men and this number was quickly diminishing. Hood's men were practically starving. They had no food, no clothes, no weapons or ammunition. Hood faced a well fed, well clothed, and fresh army at Nashville.

Nashville was not an easy city to take. It was on a commanding elevation linked by miles of entrenchments. The south side of the city had a solid arc of trenches that extended from the Cumberland River east of the city to another west of town. These were backed by a reserve line.

Hood's men deployed on the Brentwood Hills south of the city. His line was only four miles long whereas the Federal line was ten miles long. The Federal entrenchments covered all eight turnpikes which radiated southward from the city. Hood only covered four of them, the Granny White pike, the Franklin Pike toward his center, the Nolensville Pike to the east, and the Hillsboro Pike to the west. The flanks were unprotected and within his lines Hood's men were spread thin. Telegrams from Washington urged Thomas to finish the contest.

Thomas spent two weeks planning the attack and pursuit. On December 6, Lt. General Grant wired a direct order "to attack Hood at once" but Thomas ignored the order. Nine days later the Union force left the fortress city. Cheatham's Corps was on the Confederate right across the Nolensville Pike. The eastern end of the line swung forward along a railroad cut that would make it difficult for enemy attackers to approach. The center was held by Stephen Lee's Corps. This position reached from the Franklin Pike to the Granny White Pike. Stewart's Corps held the Confederate left reaching to Hillsboro Pike. Stewart's line bent back, the men building five redoubts of which only three were functional. The redoubts were small forts with four guns in each work, with fifty artillerists and one hundred infantry. The redoubts were to protect Hood's left flank, which the Federals overlapped by several miles.

On December 15, at 4:00 A.M., Thomas paid his hotel room bill and set out for the attack on Hood's army. His plan of attack was to launch an all out assault that was to begin with a feint from the Federal left, to hold the Confederate right in place, followed by a main Federal attack on the Confederate left flank of Stewart's Corps.

On the Federal left, James Steedman and his colored troops from the 1st and 2nd Colored Brigade along with two batteries rushed the Confederates and overran the railroad cut. Steedman became bogged down once he reached the Confederate works but he managed to keep Cheatham's Confederates in place all day. This charge also helped keep Stephen Lee's entire corps in the center.

On the Union right, Wilson's Cavalry pushed back Chalmer's single division of Confederate cavalry. At the same time, Andrew J. Smith pushed forward and approached Stewart's line. Confederate Brig. Gen. Matthew Ector's infantry fell back to the redoubts.

On the Federal center, Brigadier General Thomas Wood's IV Corps moved forward toward Montgomery Hill. Hood pulled back his men and the 51st Indiana took Montgomery Hill. The men of the 59th Illinois disobeyed orders and attacked the earthworks beyond Montgomery Hill. They ran three hundred yards and captured the works, including two flags and four pieces of artillery. This broke Stewart's line and the Confederates ran for the rear.

On the Confederate left only two redoubts remained at Hillsboro Pike, Redoubts No.'s 2 and 3. Farther down the pike, well to the rear of the main

Confederate artillery fire at the re-enactment of the Battle of Franklin, Tennessee.

line, were redoubts No. 4 and 5. General Walthall's division came to assist Stewart. Walthall's men were posted behind a stonewall that ran between redoubts 3 and 4. Walthall put Ector's infantry on the extreme end of the line defending the stone wall. Redoubt No. 5 fell first to General Edward Hatch's cavalry. Captain Charles Lumsden saw that No. 5 was captured and that Andrew Smith's corps was approaching. He told his men to run for their lives. The Federals now seized No. 4. Col. Slyvester Hill ordered an attack on Redoubt No. 3, where Hill was killed when a bullet went through his head but the Federals managed to take No. 3. Col. Stibbs and his 12th Iowa along with the 7th Minnesota charged and seized Redoubt No. 2.

By 1:30 P.M., Redoubt No. 1 was attacked from both sides. Stewart pulled back. As Stewart was leaving Redoubt No. 1, Brigadier General Claudius Sears was hit with a solid shot which severed his leg. As Stewart pulled back, so did Stephen D. Lee and soon Cheatham pulled back. Hood moved his army to a new position that was now only two miles long and only covered two turnpikes—The Granny White on the left and the Franklin on the right. His lines were anchored on both ends by hills. On the left was Shy's Hill and on the right was Overton Hill or Peach Orchard Hill. Hood moved Stewart's corps to the center and Cheatham to the left to cover Shy's Hill.

Cheatham's left was bent back in a great arc around the hill to protect the Confederate left flank. General Stephen Lee was on the right and fixed on Overton Hill. Hood posted his single cavalry division under Chalmer's at the end of Cheatham's line. The men began to dig in.

Two days later Thomas would attack the Confederates again. His plan was to pin down the Confederate right and overwhelm Hood's left. Col. Philip Sidney Post and his 2nd brigade and Col. Abel Streight's 1st brigade were to attack Overton Hill from the west side, while Col. Charles Thompson's black soldiers were to attack the east side of Overton Hill. Heavy canister, grape, and shell tore at the Federal troops as they climbed up the hill. On the far side of a cornfield, Federals approaching the Confederate main line came across a barrier of sharp stakes and abatis.

The 13th Colored Troops reached the Confederate breastworks and mounted the rampart. Col. Post was hit by a bullet and severely wounded and his loss stopped the Federal charge. At this moment, the Confederates poured fire into the Federals who then fell back, retreating back down the slope to the foot of Overton Hill. Hood pulled back Cleburne's division, now being led by Brig. Gen. James Smith to a crucial position on Shy's Hill. He sent the division to the right to support Lee. Lee sent Cleburne's men back but it was too late.

By early afternoon, Wilson advanced across the Granny White Pike, the Confederate line of retreat to the east. Chalmer's tried to hold off Wilson but Wilson pressed harder against the rear of Shy's Hill. The Confederates were in a vulnerable position. Ector was to defend the hill but Hood ordered Ector's men off the hill to confront Wilson's dismounted cavalry to the south. At the same time, Brig. Gen. William Bates division, of Cheatham's Corps was ordered to hold Shy's Hill.

When Cleburne's division made its shift to the right, Bate's line was stretched to the left and the defense of the hill fell to Brig. Gen. Thomas Smith's brigade.

With Smith was Col. William Shy. Shy and Smith were appalled at what they saw on the hill. Ector's men had built the breastworks in the wrong place. The Confederates couldn't cover most of the slope. The approaching Federals would be sheltered from their fire. The Confederates also had erected no abatis. When the Federals came over the crest of the hill, no more than twenty yards from the breastworks, there would be nothing to stop them.

The main attack on Shy's Hill came when General John McArthur, on his own, led his division of the XVI Corps towards the Confederate lines. Thomas saw McArthur advancing and ordered Schofield to advance his units. McArthur's three brigades proceeded under heavy fire as Schofield's men, off to the right, were going up Shy's Hill from the west. Smith's men broke the Confederate line just east of Shy's Hill and poured through the gap. On Shy's Hill, the Confederates were taking fire from the left, front and rear. Col. Shy held the line as Federal soldiers came over the crest of the hill and made for the breastworks. Shy was killed when a bullet struck him in the head. The Confederates broke and ran as Hood's lines disintegrated. Bate, Walthall, and then Brig.

Gen. Daniel Reynolds ran for their lives. Stewart and Hood had already left. On the Federal left, at Overton Hill, General Wood's troops overran the Confederate position but Lee slowly retreated in good order. On the Confederate left, General Reynolds helped Cheatham's army escape down the Franklin Pike. Darkness set in and the Federals stopped their attacks. The Battle of Nashville was over and it had cost the Union three thousand men killed, wounded or missing. The Confederates lost 6,400. In a day's fight, it wrecked and demoralized the Army of Tennessee in front of an enormous body of civilian spectators lining the hills around the battlefield. The Army of Tennessee was finished as a fighting force. The war in the West was over.

A ten-day pursuit followed, with Wilson's cavalry in the advance and Forrest's cavalry providing the rear guard from Columbia south to the banks of the Tennessee River. The last of Forrest's men crossed the river on December 27th and two days later Hood's men marched on to Tupelo, Mississippi, ending the Campaign of Franklin and Nashville. The Army of Tennessee fragmented and dispatched elements to Mississippi and Mobile, the remainder traveling east for the last campaign in the Carolina's.

The Ghosts at the Carter Plantation

A re-enactor relayed a story that happened several years ago when she traveled to the Carter Plantation. Her husband was a Civil War fanatic for years and was driving though Tennessee to visit all the battlefield sites. He planned to see the beautiful Carter Plantation house. She was not excited about seeing the house because at the time, she was not appreciative of her husband's interest in the Civil War. For her, one Civil War house was just like all the others. They were on the road all day and she just wanted to finish as soon as possible.

The Carter House became ground zero for the Battle of Franklin. After the battle, the house became a Confederate hospital, where the house became the scene of amputations and deaths. Witnesses claim the house is haunted by several ghosts. *[Etching from Battles and Leaders of the Civil War]*

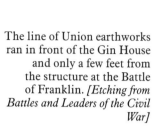

The line of Union earthworks ran in front of the Gin House and only a few feet from the structure at the Battle of Franklin. *[Etching from Battles and Leaders of the Civil War]*

They finally stopped at the Carter Plantation and purchased their tickets. As soon as they entered the house, she had an odd feeling as if she had been there before. She knew where everything was situated in the house. As the house tour began, she felt an overwhelming need to go upstairs. Her husband became annoyed with her because she broke away from the tour group and walked upstairs. Her husband asked her to stay with the tour group. She ignored his request and headed straight up the stairs.

As she reached the top floor, she quickly was drawn to one of the rooms. She entered the room and to her eyes it was transformed into an operating room. Blood was on the floor and there were two surgeons operating on patients on makeshift operating tables. The floor was covered with straw to soak up the blood that was pouring from the tables onto the floor. To her shock and terror, one surgeon was amputating an arm from a wounded Confederate soldier.

She saw other soldiers in the room. They were lined up against the walls awaiting their turn for surgery. As she looked around she saw attendants coming in and out of the room assisting the surgeons. A surgeon with a bloody white apron suddenly turned to her. He gestured for her to help out. She became fearful and panicked. As she turned to leave the room, she had a clear view out the window. There were hundreds of soldiers outside and she could hear the booming of cannons.

Just as she was about to turn for the door, her husband was standing in front of her calling out her name. At that moment, the room returned to normal. It was peaceful and quiet. Her husband was alarmed and said that she had been standing in the same position for several minutes and had not moved, even though he repeatedly called her name. She soon regained her composure and told her husband the incredible story.

Had she re-lived a past experience? Was she drawn to the room because in a past life she was one of the attendants during the battle? Or had she stepped into a window of time where only she could experience the horror of war? Did the spirits recreate the scene to make the war more real and thus force her to respect the terrible events?

The Battle of Stone's River, Tennessee

Union General William S. Rosecrans felt pressure from Washington to launch an offensive campaign against Confederate General Braxton Bragg. Washington was afraid that Bragg might attack Nashville, reinforce Confederate General Robert E. Lee or possibly outflank the Capitol and move against Union General Ulysses S. Grant. Instead, Bragg decided to wait for Rosecrans at Murfreesboro and take a defensive position. The day after Christmas, 1862, William Rosecrans with over half his army of the Cumberland advanced southeast from Nashville, Tennessee. Rosecrans attempted to fool Bragg by moving in three different directions. Thomas Crittenden came from the Murfreesboro Pike, Maj. Gen. Alexander McCook parallel to and fifteen miles west of Bragg, and Major General George Thomas was to move straight south on McCook's right, then turn east and strike the Confederate flank.[1]

The ruse worked and Bragg was confused. From December 26th to December 30th, the Yankee army moved ahead in separate columns the thirty miles to Confederate Gen. Braxton Bragg's position in front of Murfreesboro. With 38,000 men from his Army of Tennessee, Bragg was deployed along a four-mile front arching inward about 1.5 miles west and northwest of Murfreesboro. His lines covered the Nashville Pike and the winding Stone's River which passed behind his men, under the pike, and then meandered northwest along the east of the pike.[2]

Recent heavy rains raised the level of the river. Bragg put Patrick Cleburne's division on the far left, resting on the westward bend of the river with a brigade of cavalry extending south. In the woods to Cleburne's right was Leonidas Polk's Corps, extending a mile and a half across the open side of a wide eastward bend of the river, then resting on the stream. Breckinridge's division was on the east side. His left met with Polk's right across the river and extending at right angles east across the northern approach to Murfreesboro. Breckinridge was in a good position to cross the river and reinforce Polk's center but several hundred yards to his front was a commanding position called Wayne's Hill.

Rosecrans's troops skirmished daily with Bragg's cavalry and advance infantry until arriving before Bragg's main line on December 30th. Rosecrans was only a few hundred yards from Bragg's army. The Federal commander believed that if he could push Bragg from Murfreesboro, he could then secure Nashville's supply lines and eliminate threats from the Army of Tennessee until spring. Bragg hoped to do the opposite and used the days of Rosecrans's slow advance to plan the coming battle.[3]

By late on the 30th of December, facing the Confederates from right to left, he had deployed Maj. Gen. John C. Breckinridge's division, east of the pike and the river, Lt. Gen. Leonidas Polk's corps from the pike river crossing to a point about 1 1/4 mile west and Lt. Gen. William Hardee's Corps (from Polk's left and west about 1 3/4 mile). He planned to assault Rosecrans's right with Hardee's Corps and to turn the entire Union force. This would put its back to the river and cut off its northwest line of retreat on the Nashville Pike.[4]

A second road, the Wilkinson Pike, traveling west-northwest, cut the intervening ground between the Confederate left and the Nashville Pike, and intersected and ended at the Nashville Pike about a quarter of a mile behind the Southern lines. Bragg established headquarters at the intersection and ordered an attack for daylight December 31.[5]

Rosecrans's plan of battle was for McCook to hold the right, for Thomas's center troops to begin with skirmishing, Crittenden's left wing to maneuver to Stone's River and cross two divisions and then assail Bragg's right. Rosecrans's intelligence revealed that Breckinridge's lone division held the Confederate line east of the river. With two divisions to Breckinridge's one, he would thrust the Confederates back, attain Bragg's rear and flank and with the Union line wheeling to its left, push the Confederates west and southwest out and away from Murfreesboro. To ensure an overextension of the Confederate lines, he ordered McCook to send detachments farther to the left after dark on December 30th and to build campfires to give the illusion of a longer Union line. He then ordered an attack for 7:00 A.M. on December 31st.

Deceived by the false extension of Rosecrans's lines, Bragg pulled his lone reserve division, commanded by Maj. Gen. John McCown, and a second line division of Hardee's, led by Maj. Gen. Patrick Cleburne, and threw them out on his left against McCook's phantom troops. Bragg attacked at 6:00 A.M., before Rosecrans had a chance to attack and his assault caught the Federals unprepared. McCown moved forward as Cleburne put his division 500 yards behind the first line to attack Rosecrans's right flank. Willich's brigade saw the Rebels coming and fired when they got within 200 yards of the Federals. Union Brig. Gen. Edward Kirk was wounded. Willich, who was away, rode up only to be captured by the Rebels.

Rosecrans's right totally collapsed. McCown was pulled off course in his wheel movement and Cleburne had to fill in where McCown's position was located. Cleburne now faced Union Jefferson Davis's 1st brigade under Col. Sidney Post. Post couldn't handle the assault and gave way. At 7:30 A.M., the Federals reformed with fresh regiments and held until Confederate assaults broke their lines. All of Rosecrans's five brigades collapsed and Rosecrans's line was pushed a mile back on the right flank.

The Rebel assault, now hammering against McCook's left wing, pushed McCook's troops back on George Thomas. Polk forged ahead, startling the

Federals. Polk sent Cheatham's division to attack Sheridan's division, under Brig. Gen. Joshua Sill, and Brig. Gen. Jefferson Davis's Division, under Colonels William P. Carlin and William Woodruff. Woodruff was on the edge of woods on the south side of a rise. Brig. General Sill was on Woodruff's left, facing east and making a sharp angle with Woodruff's line at the top of the wooded slope. Woodruff's infantry, the 25th Illinois, 30th Illinois, and 81st Indiana with the help of the 8th Wisconsin Battery, managed to fight back attacks from Confederate infantry under Col. Loomis, comprised of the 26th, 39th, and 25th Alabama.

His right three regiments, the 1st Louisiana, 19th Alabama, and 22nd Alabama hit Sill's line. Col. Loomis was injured in the heavy fighting and his men retreated. Confederate Col. Vaughan sent in his infantry after Loomis's men fell back. Woodruff's line had taken back lost ground and fell in on their old line at Sill's right. Vaughn attacked Woodruff's battered regiments but Woodruff held and Vaughn retreated. On Loomis's right, Col. A.M. Manigault attacked Sill. Sill was killed when he was riding over to Bush's guns to aid in the advance and his men fell back on Woodruff. Woodruff was now flanked on both sides and Woodruff had no choice but to retreat. Sheridan ordered a fighting retreat.

Sheridan's men reformed their position on the Wilkinson Pike west of a farm. Brig. Gen. James Negley's division of George Thomas's center corps was linked on Sheridan's left and extended northeast toward the Nashville Pike. Sheridan's position was a cedar forest that was so dense no one could see where his men were hidden. Sheridan supplied his men with ammunition and under the cover of the forest massed 57 pieces of artillery. Sheridan's strong position now provided Rosecrans with an anchor for his right.

Rebel charge of the Union position at the Battle of Stone's River, Tennessee. *Courtesy of the Library of Congress.*

As the Federals fell back on the Nashville Pike, the first Union division sent across Stone's River to assault Breckinridge was recalled. Rosecrans moved the line of George Thomas to form another division in front of the massed artillery that Sheridan had assembled on the Nashville Pike. The Chattanooga and Nashville Railroad ran parallel to the pike on the east. Around it grew a four acre wood called the Round Forest, dubbed by soldiers "Hell's Half Acre." Rosecrans pulled his artillery to an elevation behind these woods.

Now protected from attacks from the south by Union Maj. James Negley's division, Sheridan's division held the Federal center. The Union line resembled a narrow V, its right and left being pressed back on one another. By 11:00 A.M., Sheridan's troops had fallen back, with Negley's men following quickly behind him and the new line was created with the Round Forest forming a sharp salient. The forest itself was held by five brigades under Col. William Hazen, Brig. Gen. Charles Cruft, Col. William Grose, Brig. Gen. Milo Hascall, and Col. George Wagner. Supported by the massed artillery in their rear, they withstood repeated Confederate attacks by Polk's men. Chalmers was wounded during the attack on the Round Forest and was replaced by Donelson, who was immediately attacked, but Col. William Hazen stood firm. Two brigades under Breckinridge were sent in, but the attacks were piecemeal and were not successful in dislodging the Federals from the Round Forest. Darkness ended the assaults by the Confederates. At nightfall, a thin line of Union divisions held the road to Nashville and additional troops stretched around to the east of the Round Forest facing Stone's River and Breckinridge's Confederates.

On January 1, 1863, neither side renewed the battle. Rosecrans pulled his troops from the Round Forest salient during the night, establishing a new line to the north. Still retaining some of its V shape, it covered both the Nashville Pike and the river. Bragg expected Rosecrans to retreat north on the pike and had his cavalry ready to disrupt any attempts at re-supply. After dark, January 1, 1863, Union Col. Samuel Beatty led Crittenden's 3rd Division across Stone's River and established it on a ridge facing Breckinridge.

On January 2, Confederate General John C. Breckinridge scouted the Federal lines and noticed that reinforcements and artillery were being brought up. While he was scouting, he was recalled to Bragg's Headquarters. Bragg ordered John Breckinridge to drive the Federals out of his front and back across the river. The assault would be sheer suicide and everyone knew it. Breckinridge drew on the ground with a stick and tried to explain to Bragg that the Federals were on higher ground and could sweep his men with fire from cannon and rifles. Polk and Hardee also argued against the attack. Bragg was punishing Breckinridge for not arriving in time to help out in his Kentucky Campaign in 1862. Poor railroads and politics in Knoxville kept Breckinridge in Tennessee and he was too late for the battle of Perryville.

Bragg ordered Breckinridge to assault Beatty's position and Breckinridge massed 4,500 men for the assault. He was to move his army in two lines with Hanson on the left in the first line and Gideon Pillow's brigade on the right. Col. Randall Gibson's brigade was on the left in the second line and Preston's brigade to his right. The second line formed 150 yards behind the first and served as a reserve. Each line was two regiments wide and six miles deep. Breckinridge crashed into Price's men and overran their position as Price fell back. Breckinridge now went up against the 35th, 44th, and 86th Indiana and the 30th Ohio. Breckinridge then turned off to face the 99th Ohio, 21st Kentucky and the 19th Ohio. Fyffe fell back to the low ford on the river. Grider and Price fell back before Breckinridge's powerful onslaught. The 23rd Kentucky (US) and the 24th Ohio were routed but Grose's final line tried to stop the Confederates.

The battle was observed by Union General Thomas Crittenden from a distance. Crittenden ordered his artillery chief, Maj. John Mendenhall, to mass his guns at the ford where Beatty had crossed. Breckinridge now

Union troops, in the foreground, are forced to fall back during the Battle of Stone's River, Tennessee. *Courtesy Library of Congress.*

advanced up the hill. Hanson advanced and chased Beatty across the river. The Confederate attack was supposed to stop at the heights, and then Breckinridge was to bring up his guns but his men wanted to get the battle over with and advanced further. Hanson was struck in the leg by a bullet and later died of his wounds. At 4:45 P.M., Mendenhall opened on Breckinridge with the concentrated fire of 57 cannon.

The Confederates were ripped to pieces. Breckinridge pressed on and reached a cornfield behind a hill. Union Col. Miller, of Negley's Division, was on the other side of the hill and surprised Breckinridge's men when they climbed the hill and fired a thousand rounds into Breckinridge's troops. Miller's troops then charged across the ford and by nightfall had driven Breckinridge back to his original position. On the left, the 2nd and 6th Kentucky (C.S.) followed the retreating Federals across the river. The Union brigades counterattacked across the river and Fyffe led his brigade forward. Beatty now rallied his men as Gibson retreated and the Federals took back the ridge. Soon it began to rain and darkness ended the fighting. Breckinridge soon discovered that he had lost over twenty-five percent of his division, and was heard to say, "My poor orphans! They have cut them to pieces."

Confederate Majors General Benjamin Cheatham and Withers, commanders of divisions that suffered greatly on December 31, wrote a memorandum to Bragg the night of January 2nd, asking to be allowed to retreat. Endorsed by Polk, the memorandum first angered Bragg, who rejected the idea. He reconsidered at 10 A.M., January 3, and ordered a retreat that evening, believing falsely that Rosecrans was reinforced. Left in possession of the field, Rosecrans declared Stone's River a Union victory. The stalemate cost him 1,730 dead, 7,803 wounded, and 3,717 missing. Bragg lost 1,294, 7,945 wounded, and 1,027 missing. Bragg withdrew to Shelbyville, Tennessee, while Rosecrans declined to pursue and occupied Murfreesboro instead. The Battle of Stone's River is counted as the eighth most costly battle of the Civil War.

The Buzzing of Bullets

A few years ago, Dorothy Kress described three odd encounters when she and her son visited the Stone's River battlefield. Dorothy, her husband, and children lived in Cross Plains, Tennessee. Dorothy considers herself sensitive to ghosts and spirits and often talked with her family about her visions and intuitions. It may be that her son, being immersed in her stories, considered her tales with more than a grain of salt.

Dorothy:

"I walked the land there with my son. He heard me talk often about ghosts and I told him a lot of people had experiences there. He thought I was full of it. But he had his first experience with ghosts there.

"It was November when we walked across the battlefield. My son kept swatting above his face.

"I asked him, 'Why are swatting with your hands?'

"He answered, 'I'm swatting at the flies.'

"I said, 'It's fall. There are no flies here. That is the sound of the bullets flying past your head.'

"Next he heard a cannon fire. He asked if there were re-enactors playing at battle. But there were no re-enactors that day.

"He heard a horse directly behind him and asked, 'Where's the horse?'

"I looked at him and demanded, 'What are you talking about?' Then he realized, *Oh my God it is haunted!*"

Resistance is Futile

The second story related by Dorothy Kress stated: "We all noticed something else very strange. If you were a Southerner and tried to walk on the Northern side of the battlefield there was an eerie feeling of trying to walk through thick cobwebs, a resistance to getting through. And the same effect took place for a Northerner trying to walk through the Confederate encampment. I have family members who are from different sides and they reported this happening whichever 'side' they were from. My foster daughter and my son had this happen to them. We brought her husband who is Southern. He could go into the Confederate area just fine but we couldn't.

"I also felt that when we crossed the open battlefield there was a feeling of 'come on, hurry up, you're going to get shot'. I walked really fast across that field."

Son Against Father

Dorothy Kress's third story stated: "The last time I was there with my son, I saw something really sad happen. Two soldiers stepped out of opposing woods. One was older and the other younger, one Union and the other Confederate. They drew down their rifles at each other.

"The older Federal soldier said, 'Put down your weapon! Don't make me do it. Please don't make me do it.'

"The other soldier said, 'Dad put down *your* weapon!'

"His Father said, 'No—no.'

"But the older man shot him. He shot his own son. He went over to check on the body and somebody shot him also.

"It was really sad. We both saw this happen. Later we walked into the visitor center and told someone working there that we saw a Union soldier shoot a Confederate soldier.

"I asked, 'Does anybody ever see the battle happening?'"

"She answered, 'All the time.'"

"Then I said, 'Does anybody ever mention an incident in that last field?'"

"The woman asked us, 'You mean where the Dad shot his kid? We have that scene reported to us all the time.'"

"So it was not my imagination. Even though I've lived with this psychic sensitivity all my life, I'm kind of skeptical until I get proof."

Hell's Half Acre and the Slaughter Pen

One of the most haunted areas of the Stone's River battlefield is Hell's Half Acre. In the winter of 2002, three Civil War re-enactors visited the battlefield site. As the three re-enactors left their car to walk toward Hell's Half Acre, they listened to the park's rented audiotape. The two male re-enactors followed their female companion, discussing parts of the battle. The female re-enactor was ahead by several yards checking out the flora and fauna along the trail. Suddenly she stopped walking and froze on the spot. She recalled she was unable to speak or call out. Her other two friends immediately ran to her to see why she had stopped. They looked at her terror stricken face and rushed to her aide. When they touched her, she immediately unfroze and took a deep breath.

Once she gathered her thoughts, she told them that when she walked towards Hell's Half Acre she felt a cold sensation run through her. She told them that it felt as if her breath was knocked out of her chest. She felt ready to pass out. She said she did not even notice her two companions when they approached her. She only realized where she was when they touched her. She may have stepped into the very spot where a Confederate soldier met his death as a bullet ripped through his body, taking his breath and life away.

The Battle of Bardstown, Kentucky

Terry's Texas Rangers Finest Moment

The Battle of Bardstown, Kentucky, was fought on October 4, 1862. It was lost to history, being overshadowed by a larger conflict—the battle of Perryville, which was fought on October 8, 1862. But the Battle of Bardstown was a turning point for not only the Eighth Texas Cavalry but also for Colonel John Wharton who commanded the Eighth Texas Cavalry. Of the 292 engagements led by the Eighth Texas Rangers (Terry's Texas Rangers), the Battle of Bardstown would go down as their finest moment.[1]

In late March 1861, Benjamin Franklin Terry, Thomas S. Lubbock, and John Wharton returned home from the secession convention where they were delegates. All three men agreed that they should form a regiment of Texas cavalry for the Confederate government, which was then organizing in Montgomery, Alabama. Benjamin "Frank" Terry was born in Kentucky in 1821, and taken to Brazoria County, Texas, at the age of ten. He began a sugar plantation in Fort Bend County in 1852. By 1861, Terry was regarded as one of the wealthiest men in the state.

Thomas Lubbock was born in North Carolina, in 1817 and reared in that state. He moved to Texas in 1836 with the New Orleans Grays. Lubbock was a veteran of the Texas Revolution and the Santa Fe Expedition of 1841. He was captured by the Mexicans, escaped at Mexico City, and returned to Texas in time to participate in the Somervell punitive expedition of 1842. When the Civil War broke out, Lubbock was a Houston commission merchant. His brother Francis later became governor of Texas.[2]

John Wharton was born in Nashville, Tennessee, in 1828. He was brought to Texas as an infant. He studied at the University of South Carolina. In 1861, Wharton was planning to open a law practice in Brazoria County where he was a partner with Clinton Terry, younger brother to Benjamin Terry.

In April 1861, Lubbock went to Montgomery, Alabama, to seek a commission to raise a regiment. Lubbock went away disappointed. The Confederate government felt that raising a regiment in Texas would be too costly to transport the troops and the war would be of short duration. While Lubbock was away, Wharton raised a company of cavalry in Brazoria,

Texas. Terry also raised a company in Fort Bend County and corresponded with others to assemble a regiment upon Lubbock's return. In June, the two Texans, Terry and Lubbock, were determined to get into the first big fight. They arrived in Richmond, the new Confederate capital. Terry and Lubbock made friends quickly in Richmond and both became aides on the staff of General Longstreet.

During the Battle of First Manassas, Terry and Lubbock were colonels serving under Longstreet. They were employed under the signal services. During the battle Terry and Lubbock made reconnaissance of the enemy's position. On July 21, 1861, Col. Terry rode forward under the protection of Capt. Whitehead's troops to take possession of Fairfax Courthouse. Col. Terry captured the Federal flag, said to have been made in anticipation of victory and to be hoisted over the Confederate entrenchments at Manassas. He also shot with his "unerring rifle" at the Federal flag flying on the cupola of the Fairfax courthouse. Both Col. Terry and Col. Lubbock received high praise for their "daring, and valuable reconnaissance" from Generals Beauregard and Longstreet. Terry and Lubbock again applied for a regiment of cavalry. The Confederate government gave authority for Lubbock to raise a company of cavalry.

Terry and Lubbock returned to Texas. Operating out of Houston, they recruited ten companies, mustering them into service on September 9, 1861. While at Millieau, Harrison was elected to the command of a cavalry company which was being organized for service in the Confederate army. He marched with his company to Houston, the place of his rendezvous, where it formed a part of Terry's regiment. Terry was to go to Virginia with his unit. All the Rangers were to bring their horses and equipment with them on their trip. The Rangers were not dressed in uniforms. They were wearing civilian clothing and their weapons varied immensely. They carried pistols, shotguns, rifles, twenty different calibers in all. Some of the Rangers carried as many as four revolvers.

Albert Sidney Johnston commented that the Rangers were a better armed unit than most. Pistols became a sort of money to them. The Rangers traded for items with their pistols rather than using Confederate money. The Rangers assembled in Houston. From Houston they traveled to Beaumont by foot, covering eighty miles. While at Beaumont their horses were sent home. From Beaumont they traveled by steamboat, down the Neches and up the Sabine to Niblett's Bluff. They then disembarked and walked on foot and the next forty miles they went by horse drawn carts. At New Iberia on the Bayou Teche, they were transferred to boats and went down to Brashear. From there they pushed on to New Orleans. The trip from Houston to New Orleans took one week. In New Orleans, the Rangers learned they were heading for Bowling Green, Kentucky.

On September 27, 1861, Acting Secretary of War, Judah Benjamin, sent a telegram to Albert Sidney Johnston that 1,200 men from Texas under Col.

Union Cavalry charge at the re-enactment of the Battle of Bardstown. *Courtesy of Elvin Smith, Jr.*

Lubbock were to be fully equipped, except horses. These were to be provided by Johnston. Either at Houston or en route to New Orleans, members of the command began calling themselves Texas Rangers. This mistaken notion concerning Terry's command would be a problem. The prewar reputation of the Texas Rangers would become a common assumption for Terry's Rangers. The unit would now have to live up to the former unit's reputation.

In November, the regiment's members elected Terry Colonel and Lubbock Lieutenant Colonel. At Woodsonville, Kentucky, on December 17, 1861, the regiment engaged a Federal force and Terry, leading the initial charge, was killed. Lubbock succeeded the fallen officer and the cavalrymen adopted the name Terry's Texas Rangers.

The regiment fought at the battle of Shiloh under General Nathan Bedford Forrest. They would remain under Forrest when he attacked and captured the town of Murfreesboro in July of 1862. Forrest now had 3,500 Yankees on his tail and decided to fall back to Sparta and then finally to Woodbury in the rear of the Federal force.

In the summer of 1862, Confederate General Braxton Bragg was in Chattanooga, massing his "Army of the Mississippi" and planning an

Confederate artillery's rolling thunder at the re-enactment of the Battle of Bardstown. *Courtesy of Elvin Smith, Jr.*

invasion of Kentucky. Confederate Gen. Braxton Bragg and Maj. Gen. Edmund Kirby Smith met in Chattanooga, Tennessee, on July 31st, 1862, to plan their invasion of Kentucky. Both Generals hoped to bring Kentucky into the fold of the Confederacy. Braxton Bragg had high hopes for Kentucky. Kentucky Confederate Cavalry General John Hunt Morgan promised that Braxton Bragg would be able to pick up 25,000 men if he entered this state.

Bragg was also looking for badly needed supplies. Edmund Kirby Smith was the first to enter the state in August of 1862 and was very much supported by the locals. Large crowds came out to greet him. In Lexington, Kentucky, Smith was greeted with Confederate flags waving as he entered town. The greeting would not be the same for Bragg. Bragg entered the state in areas where Union support was very high. He hoped to link up with Smith as both armies planned to march on Louisville. They tried to get to Louisville before Union General Don Carlos Buell's Army of the Ohio arrived from Knoxville, Tennessee.

Forrest left Woodbury and rode towards the Cumberland Gap, securing the road on August 29th. After capturing Yankees along the McMinnville-Murfreesboro turnpike, Forrest rode back to Sparta. Bragg told Forrest to get in the rear of Buell's army, which was retreating from Nashville. Bragg then crossed into Kentucky by the Cumberland Gap River. Forrest continued to harass Buell's rear.

At Tyree Springs, Forrest made another attack upon Buell's army. Forrest rode ten miles to the north of Buell's army to try and strike a blow to his Federal force. By accident, Forrest rode into Major General Joseph Wheeler's cavalry. Wheeler was trying to hit the Federal force upon the Nashville-Bowling Green turnpike, striking the Federal flank. Forrest tried to help Wheeler but a Federal force appeared to his right. Forrest ordered Lt. Col. Walker and his Terry's Rangers, to charge the front while Forrest moved around with the rest of the command to the Federal force's flank. Col. Walker formed his men, when to his surprise it was General Wheeler's command, falling back and in confusion. But Wheeler thought the enemy was in front of him and quickly ran away in great confusion. Forrest was getting ready to attack Wheeler when he realized what had happened. Forrest arrived at Glasgow, Kentucky, on September 8th. Forrest reported to General Bragg and Bragg told Forrest to report to General Leonidas Polk. Polk ordered Forrest to secure the Elizabethtown-Bardstown Road.

Bragg was never able to link up with Smith and ended up fighting a battle at Munfordville, Kentucky, on September 13 and 14, 1862. The battle delayed Bragg long enough to allow Union General Don Carlos Buell's army to arrive in Louisville first. While in Louisville, Buell picked up recruits and brought his army to 58,000 men. Bragg had about 15,000 men and Smith had the main army of about 25,000. Buell then secured Louisville and awaited Bragg.

Upon reaching Munfordville, Forrest learned about the Confederate victory at Munfordville. Bragg assembled his army at Munfordville and more than making a stand at Munfordville, Bragg continued on towards Bardstown. Bragg ordered Forrest to ride on to Bardstown and to secure the roads for his army.

On September 25, Forrest was ordered to General Polk's headquarters. Forrest learned that he had to head back immediately to Murfreesboro and command the new troops being formed in Middle Tennessee. This force was to harass the Yankees in Nashville. Forrest turned the command over to Col. John Wharton. Forrest took four Alabama companies with him as well as his staff. Before leaving for Murfreesboro, Forrest visited Bragg on September 27, 1862, at Bardstown and was told that the troops that Forrest was raising were to be for Bragg's command only.

Col. Wharton now commanded the brigade and Major Tom Harrison took command of the Eighth Texas Cavalry. Lt. Col. Walker, who would have been next in command, never recovered his use of the arm that was injured by a bayonet at Woodsonville, Kentucky, and had resigned in September.

On September 28, the Army of the Mississippi was put under command of General Leonidas Polk. According to Polk, Bragg ordered him to hold onto Bardstown unless a large force approached the city. He was then to fall back to Harrodsburg, Kentucky. Union General Don Carlos Buell was in Louisville, Kentucky.

By October, Buell's force was ready to move out. His army soon moved out of Louisville towards Bardstown, Kentucky. On October 4, 1862, Wharton and his men were posted four miles on the Louisville Pike, occupying and guarding the town of Bardstown and its approaches. Wharton received information that the Yankees were in force and were within a half mile to the east of the pike between Wharton and Bardstown, cutting him off from Bragg's main army.

Wharton ordered his battery to follow him as soon as possible and put himself at the head of the Rangers and rode at half speed to the point of danger. In thirty minutes, Wharton passed the four miles and then found the First and Fourth Kentucky, the Fourth Ohio, and the Third Indiana regiments of cavalry. These were four times Wharton's troop strength. They were drawn up on the road and behind some houses ready to receive him. In their rear but not in supporting distance, were a battery of artillery and a heavy force of infantry.

Union cavalry charge at the re-enactment of the Battle of Bardstown. *Courtesy of Elvin Smith, Jr.*

The Yankee cavalry was drawn up in columns of eight, prepared for a charge and the rest as a reserve. Wharton called in his outposts, threw his command into column, Rangers in front, Company D leading. The Yankees were allowed to approach within forty yards when Wharton ordered a charge. The Rangers bugle sounded the charge and they went at them as fast as their horses could carry them. The Yankees broke almost at once, firing only a few shots.

It was now a chase for several miles. The Rangers caught 200 of them and strewed the woods with their dead and wounded. Union General George Thomas, who was second in command to Buell, said that they lost twenty killed and wounded with a great many missing. The Confederates claimed that fifty were killed and forty prisoners were taken, among them a Major. If the Yankees had taken a strong position at the mouth of the lane in which the Rangers were traveling and had the Yankees had the same amount of courage as their numbers, there might have been a much different outcome. The only known casualty that the Rangers took was Private R. K. Cheatham, who was shot between the eyes during the battle. The bullet remained in Cheatham's head until he died in 1899!

After the long chase, the Rangers were scattered as much as the Union force. John Rector, seeing a lone Federal, rushed upon a Union officer and demanded his surrender.

"Surrender yourself" replied the man leveling his pistol. Rector surrendered and discharged every chamber of his pistol. Just then Bill Davis dashed up. He was a large, fierce looking man on a powerful horse not less than sixteen and a half hands high.

He broke out, "John, Why the hell don't you disarm that God d_____ Yankee?"

"I am a prisoner myself, Bill."

Quick as a flash, Davis was at the Yankee's side and bringing his pistol against his head broke out, "Give up them pistols, you___ ____ blue bellied_____ _____."

The shooting irons were promptly handed over and the prisoner escorted to the rear. It was pure bluff all around for all the firearms were empty.

Wharton was highly recognized for his bravery at the Battle of Bardstown.

General Leonidas Polk said of the Battle of Bardstown, "To this gallant action not only were the dangerous consequences of surprise obviated, but a severe chastisement was inflicted on the enemy and new luster added to the Confederate army."

Polk complimented Colonel Wharton and the brave men under him "for this daring feat of arms, (and) the general commanding could but mark the contrast with that which resulted so differently at New Harbor a short time before. Colonel Wharton and the Texas Rangers wiped out that stain. Their gallantry is worthy of the applause and emulation of their comrades of all arms in the army." For Wharton's charge at Bardstown, Confederate General Braxton Bragg, commander of the Army of the Mississippi, made Wharton a brigadier general.

Bragg would go on to fight at the Battle of Perryville on October 8, 1862, and would win a tactical victory, routing an entire corps. But it would be a strategic loss because Bragg would ultimately pull out of Kentucky and fall back to Tennessee. The major problem with Bragg's Kentucky Campaign was that it lacked a specific military objective. The Texas Rangers would also be engaged at the Battle of Perryville, fighting under General Joseph Wheeler.

The Battle of Bardstown was a victory for the Texas Rangers. The Rangers would comment for years afterwards the battle about how the battle was their finest moment. Wharton was brought to prominence for his role in the battle and the Battle of Bardstown would add new fame to the Texas Rangers.

Haunted School

Located in Bardstown, Kentucky, my Old Kentucky Home Middle School was used as a Civil War hospital. The morgue was in the basement. The floors and the ceilings have been said to bleed. The school's art room, which is also located in the basement, smells of rotting flesh. It has been said that this room was used for the holding of decomposing bodies. They painted the basement walls white, yet blood red spots bled back through the paint.

Museum with Restless Spirits

One of the fourth best Civil War museums is located in Bardstown, Kentucky. The museum contains hundreds of artifacts from Union and Confederate officers, non-commissioned officers, and enlisted men and covers ten thousand square feet. Many of the artifacts used in the museum belonged to officers who fell in battle, such as Brigadier General James S. Jackson, who was killed at the Battle of Perryville. Those who worked in the museum claim to hear voices or see someone out of the corner of their eye walk past the entrance.

One of the folding chairs contained in the artillery room moves from the wall to the center of the room. Many times the curator of the museum put the chair back against the wall. But when he entered the room in the morning to turn on the lights, the chair was once again moved away from the wall and into the center of the room.

A cleaning crew was brought in one spring to clean dust off the cases. They oiled the wood artifacts and made sure the wool uniforms did not have any damage. They also checked that the swords were free from rust. One of the cleaning crew was a woman who decided to clean the artillery room. While she was cleaning the case, a presence touched her on the shoulder. She turned around but did not notice anyone in the room with her. She shrugged her shoulders and decided to continue with her cleaning of the cases. All of the sudden, a force snapped her bra. She immediately left the building and did not re-enter.

Recently a ghost investigation team visited the museum to see if there was any validity to the claims of paranormal activity. They stayed the night in the museum but not see any apparitions. But they registered very high readings on their Electro Magnetic Field meters which could indicate a ghostly presence in the room.

Fort Duffield, Kentucky

The Civil War broke out on April 12, 1861, at Fort Sumter at Charleston, South Carolina. Kentucky soon after declared her neutrality. On September 4, 1861, Confederate General Leonidas Polk broke Kentucky's neutrality and invaded Kentucky at Columbus. The floodgates of war were open and Confederate General Albert Sidney Johnston set up his headquarters in Bowling Green, Kentucky. He arranged a defensive line stretching from Mill Springs, in Eastern Kentucky to Columbus, in Western Kentucky. Union General Ulysses S. Grant left Cairo, Illinois, and took Paducah, Kentucky.[1]

Ditto House, located in West Point, Kentucky, formerly an Inn. Stories have been told of a Confederate soldier who inhabits the house, and two sisters who died while living in the house.

Union General Robert Anderson, Kentucky native and hero of Fort Sumter, took command as Military District Commander in Kentucky with his headquarters in Louisville, Kentucky. Anderson needed to fortify Louisville and the approaches to the city. Anderson stepped down due to illness and Union General William T. Sherman took the role as military district commander. Sherman fortified West Point, Kentucky, on the confluence of the Ohio and Salt River. He ordered the 37th Indiana and the 9th Michigan to help build fortifications. Sherman planned to use West Point as a supply base for the Union troops stationed at Elizabethtown, Kentucky. Union regiments in Elizabethtown were assigned the task of protecting the Louisville and Nashville Railroad and meeting any Rebel force that moved on Louisville.[2]

Sherman chose Pearman Hill as the location for the fort. The position commanded the town of West Point and the Ohio River. In November of 1861, work began on the fort. Ten pieces of artillery from the Coldwater Michigan Battery were placed within the fort. The earthworks cover 640 feet along Pearman Hill and the distance from the top of the wall to the bottom of the ditch was seventeen feet and the top of the wall was nine feet wide. The original design of the fort was a serpentine design, with the open wall on the Ohio River.[3]

The north side of the fort was meant to protect against an invasion from Confederate forces. The fort was named in honor of the 9th Michigan's Colonel William Duffield's father, Rev. George Duffield. Soldiers constructed log cabins just outside the earthworks. During the cold winter of 1861, sixty-one soldiers died at Fort Duffield and were buried near the fort. Sherman located his headquarters in one of the nearby houses in West Point. By January 1862, the cabins and the fort were complete and 950 soldiers took residence in the fort.

By the end of January 1862, the Union army abandoned the fort. The Union army moved into Tennessee and Mississippi. In the fall of 1862, Confederate General Braxton Bragg's Army of the Mississippi and Confederate General Edmund Kirby Smith's Army of East Tennessee invaded Kentucky. Bragg hoped to capture Louisville, Kentucky. Smith had taken Lexington and Kentucky's state capitol, Frankfort. When Union General Don Carlos Buell heard of Bragg's invasion, he left Alabama and turned his Army of the Ohio towards Kentucky. On September 25, 1862, Buell's tired and hungry men reached West Point, Kentucky. Six gunboats arrived at West Point and forty thousand Union troops entered the small Kentucky town. Six steamboats from Louisville arrived with a million rations to the army station in West Point. After Buell's men ate their rations, they moved onto Louisville and secured the city against Bragg's army.

After the Battle of Perryville, on October 8, 1862, the Union army continued to move south and pushed the Rebels back into Tennessee. Fort Duffield was no longer needed by the Union army and fell into disrepair. West Point continued to see guerilla activity from Confederate guerilla Ben Wiggington.

Angry Sentry

John Wiedeburg stated in his story:

A friend and I were camping out at Fort Duffield south of Louisville. We were on top of the parapet of the Fort at night when he took some flash photos. Apparently that angered the ghost sentry up there.

He attacked all three of us. He bit Janine (Bennett) in the legs and clawed my legs. And it looked like he took a pocketknife to cut Mat's legs. We all saw the teeth marks on Janine's legs. We saw blood on Mat's legs. It was odd, just sort of appeared. There was no way the cuts were caused by grass or sticks because the grass was cut low to only two inches. We couldn't figure out any rational explanation for the bites and cuts.

Monument dedicated to the Union dead that died at Fort Duffield, south of Louisville, Kentucky.

Earthen walls of Fort Duffield, Hardin County, Kentucky.

In addition, we saw all night long what looked like flashes going off up on the parapet. It went on until about three o'clock in the morning. Later we noticed a big orb in the digital image.

Built in 1841, the Ditto House served as a Union officers quarters during the Civil War. The Ditto-Lansdale House served as a Civil War hospital.

During the 1990s, the Ditto house served as a bed and breakfast. Guests claimed to see two women in black mourning dresses that would check on them in their rooms. The ghosts are claimed to be two sisters who lived in the house. Guests also saw a Confederate soldier in the kitchen. The house also experiences poltergeist type behavior. During the Fort Duffield preservation meeting in the Ditto House, the lights went out downstairs but all the lights upstairs remained on. The owner of the Ditto House Inn told everyone to keep calm and the lights would soon come on.

The owner called out in a loud voice, "Ok, that's enough."

As soon as he bellowed out his words, the lights came back on in the house as if nothing had happened. The owner said that the ghost of the house enjoys turning the lights on and off.

Camp Nelson, Kentucky

Camp Nelson, located in Jessamine County, was one of the largest recruitment camps for African American soldiers. The United States government recruited eight regiments of the United States Colored Troops and three other black regiments trained at Camp Nelson. Camp Nelson also established a refugee camp for the black soldiers' families. Camp Nelson served as an important Union quartermaster and commissary depot, recruitment center, and hospital facility. Camp Nelson provided supplies, livestock, and troops for the Union Army of the Ohio.[1]

In June 1863, Union General Ambrose Burnside, commander of the Army of the Ohio, ordered the construction of Camp Nelson. Burnside wanted a secure supply depot and encampment for his planned campaign to capture Knoxville, Tennessee. The Union government named Camp Nelson after Union General William "Bull" Nelson, founder of Camp Dick Robinson, which became the first Union recruitment camp in Kentucky.

During the Civil War, the Oliver Perry House was commandeered by the Union army and used as quarters by the Quartermaster and Commissary officers, including Chief Quartermaster Captain Theron F. Hall. Camp Nelson, Jessamine County, Kentucky.

The Union army built three hundred buildings, numerous tents, and nine forts. The center of the camp covered eight hundred acres on either side of the Lexington-Danville Turnpike. Twenty warehouses contained two million rations, clothing, equipment, stables, cribs, barns, sheds, corrals for thousands of mules, horses, and their feed. Six industrial sized workshops built and repaired wagons and ambulances, made and repaired harnesses, shod horses, and provided lumber for construction. Two ordnance warehouses and a large powder magazine housed cannons, small arms, ammunition, and powder.[2]

Administrative buildings included the camp headquarters, quartermaster and commissary office, provost marshal's office, and other small offices. A large hospital, with ten wards, a "Soldier's home," and a prison completed the camp. The army also constructed two barracks, two taverns, sutler stores, many mess houses, and a bakery. The bakery produced ten thousand rations of bread per day. During the Civil War, many homes did not have running water but Camp Nelson built a water works, in which a steam

Graveyard No.1. The monument is dedicated, "To those buried here. Here lie the bodies of numerous unknown Tennessee white refugees and Kentucky African American refugees who perished from disease while at Camp Nelson." These civilians sought freedom and protection within the U.S. Army Post.

engine pumped 150 gallons of water per minute up nearly five hundred feet from the Kentucky River through twenty thousand feet of lead pipe to the hospitals, soldiers' homes, and machine shops.

The government employed over two thousand civilians, including carpenters, blacksmiths, wagon makers, harness makers, teamsters, cooks, clerks, laborers, and many impressed slaves. Between three thousand to eight thousand soldiers garrisoned at Camp Nelson. The camp also became a staging ground and supply center for three important campaigns—Major General Ambrose Burnside's August-November 1863 Campaign, Major General Stephen Gano Burbridge's October 1864 Southwestern Virginia Campaign, and Major General Burbridge's wing of Major General Stoneman's December 1864 Southwestern Virginia Campaign. During the three years Camp Nelson was in operation, about eighty thousand Union soldiers passed through the camp.

Camp Nelson recruited the 47th and 49th Kentucky Mounted Infantry, Battery E of the 1st Kentucky Light Artillery, Companies K through E of the 8th Tennessee Infantry, the 8th Tennessee Cavalry, Companies B and C of the 9th Tennessee Cavalry, Companies A and D of the 11th Tennessee Cavalry, and Batteries B and E of the 1st Tennessee Light Artillery.

In 1864, Camp Nelson became an important recruitment station for black regiments. After the Emancipation Proclamation, a flood of slaves and free blacks arrived at Camp Nelson. The black recruits sought their freedom and wished to fight for the liberation of their fellow enslaved brothers and sisters. By the end of 1865, ten thousand men or forty percent of Kentucky's black soldiers, passed through Camp Nelson. Camp Nelson formed the 114th, 116th, 119th, and the 124th United States Colored Infantry; the 5th and 6th U.S. Colored Cavalry; and the 12th and 13th U.S. Colored Heavy Artillery Regiments. The 115th, 117th, and the 123rd U.S. Colored Infantries were also stationed at Camp Nelson.

Many of the black regiments recruited at Camp Nelson saw action during the Civil War. At the Battle of Saltville, the 5th and a portion of the 6th U.S. Colored Cavalry fought Confederate forces under General John C. Breckinridge. The first battle of Saltville ended with a Confederate victory and unfortunately after the battle, forty-five of the wounded and captured black soldiers and one of the white officers commanding the black regiments were shot to death by Confederate forces.

Unfortunately, a larger number of deaths of blacks did not occur on the battlefield. In November 1864, Union General Speed S. Fry, commander of Camp Nelson, ordered four hundred black refugees out of the camp on a bitterly cold day. The government countermanded Fry's order, but the damage had already been done and 102 refugees died from exposure and disease. The political uproar over the death of the black refugees led to the February 1865 Congressional Act which freed the families of the black recruits and led to the establishment of a home for the refugees.

In June 1866, Camp Nelson finally closed its doors. Abisha Scofield, John G. Fee, and Gabriel Burdett of the American Missionary Association bought the school at Camp Nelson and other administrative buildings and the cottages continued to be inhabited by black families. Ariel College, founded by John G. Fee, was a forerunner to Berea College and many of the students taught at Ariel College at Camp Nelson followed Fee to Berea.

In 1866, the main Camp Nelson cemetery became a National Cemetery. The original cemetery contained 1,615 soldiers, including 837 United States Colored Troops and even some civilian employees who died at Camp Nelson. In the summer of 1868, 2,203 Union dead from the Battle of Perryville, Richmond, Frankfort, London, and Covington were re-interred at the Camp Nelson National Cemetery.

Camp Nelson National Cemetery. In June and July of 1868 over 2,000 Union dead were removed from five areas of Kentucky and reburied at Camp Nelson Cemetery, including 975 bodies from the Battle of Perryville.

African-American workers standing on railroad tracks in front of a storage facility.
Courtesy of the Library of Congress.

This home in central Kentucky was given to a young couple as a wedding gift about 140 years ago. When the groom was called away to serve in the Civil War, his bride told him she would not leave the window until he returned. The soldier arrived home a few years later and he was told that his wife had become ill and died in her sleep. He closed the window and died in the same room of a broken heart.

Today, the shutters of that window cannot be opened. The ghosts are also said to cause many traffic accidents in the area. Other stories that circulate around the home pertain to a man who hung himself in the house; his ghost can be seen from the window. After the Battle of Perryville, the home was used as a Civil War hospital and the location of the home is near Camp Dick Robinson, which was the first Union recruiting camp in Kentucky.

Forrest's First: The Battle of Sacramento, Kentucky

The Battle of Sacramento, Kentucky, was a turning point in the career of Confederate Nathan Bedford Forrest. The battle would hone Forrest's fighting skills, which would win him great fame in the battles of Shiloh, Brice's Crossroads, and many other engagements. Although this battle has been largely ignored, it would go down as Forrest's beginning.[1]

Before the Civil War broke out, Nathan Bedford Forrest lived in Tennessee and became a wealthy slave trader and plantation owner, amassing a fortune of $1,500,000 dollars. When the Civil War broke out, Forrest joined the Confederate army as a private in Josiah H. White's cavalry company on June 14, 1861. In October of 1861, Forrest, at his expense, raised his own regiment of cavalry. In the second week of October, elections were held for officers and Forrest was made Lieutenant Colonel and Capt. D. C. Kelley was made Major.[2]

The regiment was ordered to Fort Donelson, but Confederate General Lloyd Tilghman ordered Forrest's command to Hopkinsville, Kentucky, which he reached on November 21, 1861. While in Hopkinsville, Forrest's command was increased to ten companies. On December 1st, Forrest wanted to make a reconnaissance with his command to check out the Federal forces near Calhoun, Kentucky, on the north bank of the Green River. It was rumored that Kentucky native Union General Thomas Crittenden, and 10,000 infantry and 1,200 cavalry were assembling in that area.[3]

Permission was granted and Forrest with 450 men started out for Calhoun. After the reconnaissance was made, Forrest returned to Hopkinsiville, and started to build huts for his men to wait out the winter. While Forrest and his men were beginning to settle in at Hopkinsville, there was a rumor that Federals were moving towards the Confederate lines.[4]

Forrest was ordered to make another reconnaissance for definite confirmation of the Federals movements. On December 26, Forrest took 300 of his men in the direction of the Green River, by the way of Greenville, Muhlenburg County. The roads were muddy and iced over, so Forrest stopped and assembled his men at Greenville. He then decided to reconnoiter the road toward Rumsey, directly opposite to Calhoun, where it was understood that General Crittenden and his forces were stationed.[5]

On the morning of the 28th, it was rumored that a detachment of Federal cavalry, some 500 strong, had crossed Calhoun that morning to the south side of the river at Rumsey. Excited about the prospect of engaging the Federals, Forrest and his men quickly rode to a small town called Sacramento. As

Forrest approached Sacramento, a beautiful young lady on horseback, by the name Miss Morehead, rode up to Forrest and told him that a Federal force was just in front. Forrest said that the young girl "infused nerve into my arm and kindling knightly chivalry within my heart."

One mile before entering Sacramento, Forrest's advance guard came upon the rear guard of Major Murray's 168 men, of Jackson's regiment, who were returning from a reconnaissance in South Carrollton, Kentucky. Murray's men stopped to see if the force coming up on them was friend or foe. Forrest quickly pulled out his Maynard rifle and fired at the Yankees. The Yankees rode off rapidly to their column. The column then moved up a wooded ridge and formed right angles to the road just over its brow.[5a]

Forrest ordered up the head of his column, telling his men to hold their fire until within good range. The Yankees started to fire when Forrest's 150 men were within 200 yards. When Forrest and his men got to within 120 yards, he ordered his men to fire. After three rounds were fired, Forrest noticed that he did not have enough men to take the Yankee position, so he ordered his men to fall back. The Yankees tried to flank their left, and moved towards Forrest's men, thinking that Forrest was in retreat.[5b]

The Yankees moved down 100 yards and formed for a charge when the rest of Forrest's command came up. Forrest ordered some of his men, who were equipped with Sharp's carbines and Sharp's and Maynard rifles, to dismount and act as sharpshooters. He ordered Major Kelley and Col. Starnes to make a flank movement of the right and left of the Yankees. With the detachments from the companies under Forrest's command, who were still mounted, Forrest ordered them to charge the Yankees. The men sprang to the charge with a shout. The Yankees poured a sharp fire into the oncoming Confederates, and during this charge Capt. Merriwether, next to Forrest, was shot in the head with two bullets and fell from his horse.[5c]

The Yankees were broken by the charge and seeing that they were being outflanked, one of the Union men panicked and yelled out "Retreat to Sacramento!"

The Yankees ran for their lives, scattering in all directions. They chased the Yankees into Sacramento, where the best of Forrest's men came up behind the Yankees and a saber fight broke out, which lasted for two miles beyond the town. The Yankees threw down their arms and rode with all the speed they could muster, and rode as fast as they could away from Forrest's oncoming men and back to the main force stationed at Camp Calhoun under Union General Thomas Crittenden.

Forrest and his mounted men ordered the fleeing Yankees to surrender. The Yankees refused and kept on riding at a break neck speed. Some of Forrest's men, who managed to catch up with the fleeing Yankees, pierced through every soldier they came upon. Three miles outside of Sacramento, Forrest rode too far forward of his men and became engaged in a hand to hand conflict with two Federal officers and a private. Forrest shot the private through his collar. The Union officers, Capt. Bacon and Davis assaulted Forrest with their sabers.

Forrest quickly bent his body forward to elude the thrusts of the sabers. The sword points only touched Forrest's shoulder. At one point, Forrest thrust his saber into Capt. Albert Bacon, and Capt. Arthur Davis was thrown from his horse when Forrest hit him with a heavy blow to his sword arm. Both officers fell from their horses, and Capt. Davis dislocated his shoulder from the fall, and later surrendered. Capt. Bacon was killed. Both horses were now dismounted and ran into each other and were knocked over the bottom of a short, abrupt hill. Forrest came upon these two horses and he, along with his horse fell to the earth. Forrest flew for twenty feet until he landed among the two horses that caused the fall. Some of the Yankees also encountered the fallen horses, and were thrown from their mounts. They were too exhausted to get up, so they remained near their fallen horses and were later taken prisoner.

Forrest, who was not injured by the fall, noticed that the Federals were out of sight and their camp was only three miles away. As his men were becoming disorganized, he called off the chase. Upon returning to Sacramento, Forrest found dead and wounded in every direction. Those who were able to move were placed in wagons. Capt. Burgess and Davis were taken to the nearest farm house, so their wounds could be looked after by the local townspeople.

Forrest estimated 65 killed and wounded and 35 Union prisoners were taken, for a loss of 100 Yankees. Forrest reported that Capt. Merriwether, and Private William H. Terry, of Capt. McLemore's company were killed. During the battle, Private W. H. Terry was riding with his commanding officer, and became engaged in a single-handed conflict with Union Captain Arthur Davis. Terry began to hit the Yankee with his rifle, when he was run through by Capt. Davis. Terry fell from his horse dead. Three privates were slightly wounded. Two were from Capt. May's company and the other was from Capt. Hambrick's. Forrest returned to Greenville, and then to Hopkinsville.

This battle was important not only for the success and confidence it inspired in Forrest's raw cavalrymen, but also it displayed Forrest's characteristics and natural tactics, which were subsequently more fully developed. He showed a reckless courage in making the attack, which intimidated his enemy. He commanded a quick dismounting of his men to fight, showing that he regarded horses mainly as a rapid means of transportation for his troops.

In addition, Forrest's intuitive adoption of the flank attack so demoralized the enemy, even in the open field and much more so when made, as Forrest often did, under cover of woods that concealed the weakness of the attacking party. He displayed a fierce and untiring pursuit which so often changed retreat into rout and made victory complete. He always was in front, making personal observations and sending back orders for moving his troops, "while his keen eye watched the whole fight and guided him to weak spots. This practice brought him into many personal conflicts and exposed him to constant danger. This practice often led to imitation by his general officers.

Strange Photos from Sacramento Battlefield Homestead

John Wiedeburg related his story of Sacramento:

We participated in the Sacramento (Kentucky) Civil War Re-enactment in May of 2008. The battle was of course in December but the re-enactment is held in nicer weather on the third weekend in May. We arranged with the City of Sacramento to tour the historic battlefield homestead. It was built in the 1830s. More recently it was moved to Hwy 81 in McLean County, Kentucky. It is a beautiful two-story log cabin, which was donated to the city.

There were five of us who signed up for the nighttime tour. When the tour got going, it was nearly 10:30 P.M. because eighty-five people showed up! We knew that Col. Nathan Bedford Forrest had used the homestead to set up his field command. We felt some kind of spirit presence in the old home despite large numbers of folks touring that night in shifts. We didn't run our cassette recorders but we do like to try to capture evidence of ghosts. Our ghost investigation business is titled "Singing Cat Paranormal Investigations."

When we later looked at the print photographs from that night we found over a half dozen pictures with very odd lights streaked across the image. These unexplained lights were mostly orange with one white. They were not hazy or misty but rather seem to occur near the folks on tour, like Janine and a few others.

We heard that a restaurant that once stood next door had burnt down. And perhaps the house has resident ghosts since Civil War times. But the spirits we felt and the evidence from photographic anomalies could be the ghosts of Civil War soldiers from the Battle of Sacramento.

Unexplained light in the second floor of the Sacramento, Kentucky, historic Homestead House. *Courtesy of John Wiedeburg.*

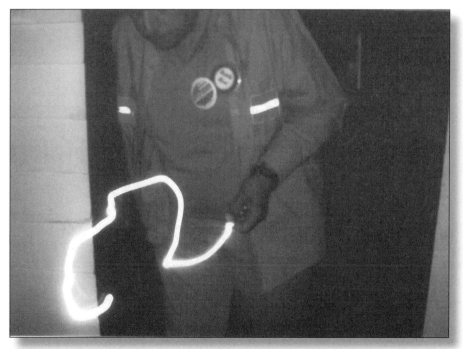

Unexplained light extending from the small flashlight of a tourist at the Sacramento, Kentucky, historic Homestead House. *Courtesy of John Wiedeburg.*

Other Tales of
Civil War Ghosts

Fort Pillow

One of the worst massacres and a controversial event during the Civil War took place at Fort Pillow, Tennessee. Fort Pillow was an earthwork fort located on a high bluff overlooking the Mississippi River forty miles north of Memphis, Tennessee. It was one of the many garrisons the Union army used to protect their supply lines. At Fort Pillow, the Union army placed 295 white soldiers from the 13th (U.S.) Tennessee Cavalry and 265 black soldiers from the 11th U.S. Colored Troops and Battery F, 4th United States Colored Light Artillery. The tin clad gunboat *New Era* covered the fort's riverfront.[1]

African-American soldiers guard bomb proof headquarters. *Courtesy of the Library of Congress.*

During the month of April, Confederate General Nathan Bedford Forrest sent a message to his superiors.

He wrote: "There is a federal force of 500 or 600 at Fort Pillow which I shall attend to…As they have horses and supplies which we need."

On April 12, 1864, at 5:30 A.M., Confederate General Forrest's 1,500 men, under the command of Brigadier General James Chalmers, attacked the fort. The Union force's six cannons could not place Chalmer's men into the range of their guns and neither could the guns from the gunboat. Chalmer's men pushed the Federal soldiers from the entrenchments into the fort's interior earthworks. At 10 A.M. Forrest arrived and placed his men in strategic positions where they could fire down on the fort.

At 11 A.M. Forrest's men took the Federal barracks on the fort's south side and fired from the cover of the barracks into the fort's south side. Forrest's men poured deadly fire into the fort and at 3:30 P.M. Forrest ordered his men to cease-fire and sent a flag of truce and demanded that the Federal force surrender. Major Lionel F. Booth, commander of the fort, could not surrender the fort because Forrest's sharpshooters killed him earlier in the day. The second in command, Major William F. Bradford, requested an hour to consult with his officers.[2]

Bradford hoped that his stalling tactic would last long enough for Union reinforcements to arrive on transport boats. Forrest could see the smoke billowing from the transports' smoke stacks and discovered Bradford's ploy. He gave Bradford only twenty minutes to decide to surrender. At the end of twenty minutes, Forrest ordered his men to resume their attack on the fort. The Confederates charged the last Union line of works and drove the Federals over the bluff and down the riverbank and into Confederate Captain Anderson's men. Many of the Union soldiers tried to surrender.

What happened next remained controversial. The Confederates lost 14 killed and 86 wounded and captured 226 federals, killed 231, and wounded 100 soldiers. Some of the Union soldiers claimed that as Confederates scaled the earthworks they yelled out racial slurs and killed black soldiers who had thrown down their arms to surrender. Other Union soldiers claimed that Forrest's men killed wounded Union soldiers, both black and white. Confederates claimed the high casualty rates came when the survivors of the fort ran, fighting their way to the river.

Some Confederates claimed that the black soldiers picked up their arms again after surrendering and paid the ultimate price for not abiding by the surrender terms. Other accounts placed the high casualty rate among the blacks on their steadfast defense of the earthworks, claiming that the black soldiers were the last to abandon the fort. After the battle, Forrest only had 58 black Union soldiers taken prisoner out of the 262 engaged during the battle. After the engagement, Forrest claimed the battle of Fort Pillow was not a massacre. One point cannot be disputed. Many of the Forrest's men, who were from Tennessee, considered the soldiers of the 13th Tennessee

Cavalry, U.S., traitors or renegades. Many Confederates would not take black Union soldiers prisoner and their commanding white officers would be shot if captured. Another massacre occurred in 1864 at the Battle of Saltville, Virginia, in which Confederate soldiers, including the infamous guerilla Champ Ferguson, massacred wounded black soldiers from the 5th and 6th United States Colored Cavalry.

African-American troops.
Courtesy of the Library of Congress.

According to Civil War re-enactors who have camped at Fort Pillow, a shadow person inhabits the grounds of Fort Pillow. Many ghost researchers claim that malevolent spirits called shadow people haunt some sites. Re-enactors claim that while they were walking the parking lot, they would feel as if they were being watched and when they turned around to see if anyone was following them, they would not see anyone there.

However, when they looked down at their shadows, they would not only see their own shadows, but also another dark shadow trailing behind them. Other Confederate re-enactors have claimed that a force would push them or trip them, causing many re-enactors to twist an ankle. Could this be the spirit of one of the black Union soldiers who were massacred, taking his revenge on the unsuspecting Confederate re-enactors?

The Box and the Sword

Pam Downs

My first encounters with the ghost started when we brought home a rocking chair. It came from a Civil War mansion, which my father was wrecking. He demolished buildings for an apartment complex that was being built. When the rocking chair came home we started seeing strange things happen at our house. We brought the rocking chair with us to where we live now. We also had it in our old house on Spring Street, in New Albany, Indiana.

Our daughter Janna had an experience this morning, which is the first since we've lived here. We do know also that a woman died in this house so we're not sure if our ghosts are the same or if this is a different spirit. We have been awakened many times in this house. It generally happens when one of us is here alone. I've heard "Mom." I've also heard shouting, "Get up!" That jarred me right out of bed.

My dad, Raymond Lawson, brought home the rocker. He also brought home a large wooden box that was full of iodine, Mercurochrome, and other medicines we didn't recognize. It had extremely large, beaker-type bottles, flasks, and lots of chemistry-type bottles. The bottles were like pharmaceutical types of things but larger. In fact, I've got one upstairs. He brought this stuff home and I wanted the box. I put the old wooden box in my bedroom. And it was really funny because—now, my earlier encounter happened with the rocking chair.

The mansion was in Louisville, maybe on Hurstbourne Parkway. I know that they tore it down and built a large apartment complex. I remember at the time they gave the woman $100,000 for the house. He talked about the mantles. The fireplaces were so big you could literally walk into them. He said she laid the check on the mantle. When they came back she was still in the house. She was supposed to have moved out.

They told her they were going to start razing the house and she reached up and got the check that had been there for months. She asked them to take it back—she didn't want to sell her house. This was during the 1960s, because a lot of the house that my parents lived in and where all of this occurred—the wood, door frames, and trim came from the house—a lot of the stuff was salvaged. And that's part of what my dad did. But he kept the rocking chair and the box. This woman's grandfather had been a doctor during the Civil War when he treated patients at that mansion. He had an office somewhere in the house.

The rocking chair and the upholstery that was on it had blood all over it. So my dad set it out on the front porch. Well, that rocking chair disappeared. We found out later that the lady who lived next door—he did some work for her and gave her some things—had taken it. My father thought somebody had stolen it.

Well, a couple weeks later the neighbor came and got him and told him to come over to her house. She had re-upholstered the rocking chair. She took off the bloody fabric and put on cranberry velvet. That's what was on it when my dad brought it home and put it in our living room. When my husband and I moved to our house on Spring Street, we took the rocking chair and wooden box with us. We would hear footsteps upstairs. And for years the upstairs wasn't finished. That house also had someone die in it.

And then I had the box in my bedroom.

I think I was eleven or twelve years old. It was in the 1960s...I remember it was around Christmas and my mother always would, after she put up the Christmas tree and the presents, plug in the tree. So when we woke up we saw the glow of Christmas lights and we knew Santa had been there. It was an exciting time. This was a day or two before Christmas.

I woke up, you know how kids are—I had gone to bed anticipating Christmas. I woke up and I saw the glow, forgetting it was not yet Christmas. I had to go to the bathroom and I thought, "Santa's been here." I might have been younger because I was thinking about Santa. I got up and I went down and I heard voices. So I snuck on up and when I did, there were three people in the room and one of them was sitting in the rocking chair and the other two were standing.

Soldier's portrait. *Courtesy of the Library of Congress.*

And we had this big old fireplace and my father had two Civil War swords, one from the Mansion. The swords were hanging on the fireplace. One guy had on a huge, odd hat and they were just there. The brim on his hat was all rolled up. I walked into the room and they all turned and looked at me and they shouted at me to get out and go back to bed. They had a glow but then the glow became lighter like they were going away. But I had really ticked them off. I interrupted a private conversation. I was so afraid, I ran down the hall and I got in my bed and I covered up and I shook and I shook. I couldn't go back to sleep, I remember that. I was so afraid they were going to come and get me.

I had the box in my bedroom, this was years later. When I opened up the box and leaned it against the wall, it nearly hit me in the head. I can't tell you how many times. We're talking a lid that's open, leaning, and it slammed shut! It just missed my face two or three times.

I had, as my mother called it, my "hopeless" chest. That's what that was, I was always putting things in the box but it would always slam on me. I would pull it out again from the wall so I could lean it—that was the thing, how come it would close on me?

Civil War Spirit Comes with Sword

Recently a Civil War collector told the author, Bryan Bush, about a set of circumstances surrounding the purchase of an original Confederate officer's sword. The family, who originally owned the sword, fell on hard times and decided to sell the sword. The sword was in really good condition, except for bloody stains on the blade. After negotiating a price, the Civil War collector bought the sword from the family. Once the collector took the sword home, odd occurrences began to happen in his house. The toilets would mysteriously flush or the water faucets in the bathroom would turn on by themselves. The family of the Civil War collector could not get any sleep because the incidents became more and more frequent in the night. The lights in the house began to turn on by themselves, and the new owner of the sword began to believe that the Confederate officer's sword could have brought the soul of its original owner into the house. The collector sold the sword to another collector and soon after the sword left his house, the incidents disappeared and the house returned to normal.

The Vicksburg Campaign

In late 1862, Union General Ulysses S. Grant set his sights on Vicksburg, Mississippi. Vicksburg was a strategic location because it controlled the center of the Mississippi River. It was a transfer point for both rail and river traffic headed east toward the heart of the Confederacy. It was also one of the few rail links to the West. Vicksburg was not going to be easy to take, as it was situated on a series of discouraging bluffs above the river. The fortifications rose 300 feet above the river and protected the city from any attack from that direction. The surrounding areas were swamps and bogs. East of the city, the line of bluffs fell away to a plain, and hillsides commanded the eastern approaches. General Grant made several attempts to take Vicksburg.

Following failures in the First Vicksburg Campaign, the battle of Chickasaw Bluffs, the Yazoo Pass Expedition, and Steel's Bayou Expedition, in the spring of 1863 Grant prepared to cross his troops from the west bank of the Mississippi River to a point south of Vicksburg and drive against the city from the south and east. Commanding Confederate batteries at Port Hudson, Louisiana, farther south, prevented the transportation of waterborne supplies and any communication from Union forces in Baton Rouge and New Orleans.

Naval support for his campaign would have to come from Rear Admiral David Porter's fleet north of Vicksburg. Running past the powerful Vicksburg Batteries, Porter's vessels, once south of the city, could ferry Federals to the east bank. There the infantry would face two Confederate forces, one under Lt. Gen. John C. Pemberton at Vicksburg and another around Jackson, Mississippi, soon to be commanded by Joseph Johnston.

In January 1863, Grant organized his force into the XIII Corps under Major General John McClernand, the XV Corps under William Tecumseh Sherman, the XVII Corps under Major General Stephen Hurlbut, and the XVII Corps under Major General James McPherson. Simultaneous with Grant's Vicksburg offensive, Major General Nathaniel Banks began his maneuvering along the Red River in Louisiana.

Hurlbut's Corps was subsequently transferred to New Orleans. With his remaining corps, Grant began operations late in March. On March 29 and 30, 1863, McClernand's and McPherson's men at Milliken's Bend and Lake Providence, northwest of Vicksburg, began working their way south. They built a military road to New Carthage, Louisiana, and prepared to move south to Hard Times, Louisiana, which was a village opposite Bruinsburg, Mississippi.

On the night of April 16, 1863, at Grant's request, Porter took twelve vessels south past the Vicksburg batteries, losing one to Confederate fire. On April 17, 1863, Grierson's Raid began. Led by Brigadier General Benjamin Grierson, Federal cavalry left for Louisiana from Grange, Tennessee. For sixteen days Grierson rode through central Mississippi to Baton Rouge, Louisiana, pulling away large units from Vicksburg's defense to pursue them. On the night of April 22, 1863, Porter, encouraged by light losses on his first try, ran a large supply flotilla past the Vicksburg batteries. Sherman's troops, many at work on the canal project at Duckport, abandoned this work and joined in a last action along the Yazoo River, northeast of Vicksburg.

On April 29-30, 1863, Sherman moved towards the Confederate works at Haynes Bluff and Drumgould's Bluffs, diverting more of Pemberton's force. Also on April 29, 1863, as McClernand's and McPherson's troops gathered near Hard Times, Porter's fleet assailed Confederate batteries at Grand Gulf, thirty-three miles southwest of Vicksburg, testing the Grand Gulf area as a landing site for Union troops. Though Porter found the guns there too strong, he had succeeded in further diverting Pemberton from Vicksburg.

Grant originally determined that Rodney, Mississippi, would be the starting point of his invasion, but took the advice of a local slave and picked Bruinsburg instead. On April 30, 1863, McClernand's and McPherson's corps were ferried east across the Mississippi from Hard Times. On that same day Grant sent word north for Sherman to follow McPherson's route and join him.

On May 1, 1863, the Federal invasion force engaged the Confederates in the battle of Port Gibson. Pemberton had just over forty thousand men assigned to the Vicksburg region. Since they were scattered throughout the area, chasing Grierson and wary of Sherman, few of them could be brought to bear against Grant on short notice. Defeated at Port Gibson, Pemberton's troops moved north. Grant, to Pemberton's confusion, pushed northeast. On May 8, 1863, Sherman's corps joined him and five days later, on May 12, 1863, Union and Confederate forces fought at Raymond. Johnston sent Brigadier General John Gregg to move up through Jackson and then march west for fifteen miles to Raymond. Gregg was to attack Grant's flank and rear. Pemberton didn't know that Grant was also marching on Jackson. McPherson's XVII Corps, ten thousand men strong, was in the lead and Gregg's brigade was in its path.

Gregg attacked thinking McPherson's force was small. Gregg sent the 7th Texas and 3rd Tennessee south across 14 Mile Creek to pin down the Federals, while four other regiments forded the creek to the east and hit McPherson's right flank. The Texans and Tennesseans launched a furious attack, slamming into the 23rd Indiana. Panic spread among the Federals because the dense woods would not allow them to form up or fix bayonets. Major General John Logan, commander of the 3rd Division, rallied the men and launched an attack and the Confederates were driven back across the creek. By the time Gregg launched his attack on the flank, Logan was in command along the creek. Decimated by fire in front and flank, the Confederates faltered, then fell back. By 2 P.M., Gregg retreated toward Raymond. The Federals lost 442 men. The Confederates lost 514. Gregg abandoned Raymond and headed for Jackson.

On May 13, 1863, Johnston took personal command of the Confederates at Jackson, fifteen miles northeast of Raymond. Johnston was cut off from Pemberton's forces, so he left Brigadier General W.H.T. Wallace and Colonel Peyton Colquitt astride the Clinton Road and assigned the 3rd

Kentucky Mounted Infantry and some sharpshooters to guard the southwest approach to Jackson. On May 14, 1863, Federals under Brigadier General Marcellus Crocker and Brigadier General William Tecumseh Sherman, with four regiments under Colonel Samuel Holmes's brigade, attacked, and quickly won an engagement at Jackson. Federal losses were three hundred men and Gregg lost two hundred men. Sherman and Crocker had cut off Johnston from Pemberton and ensured the latter's isolation for the rest of the campaign. In two weeks, Grant's force had come well over 130 miles northeast from their Bruinsburg landing site.

Ordering Sherman to destroy Jackson's heavy industry and rail facilities, Grant turned west, roughly following the Southern Mississippi railroad to Bolton. On May 14, 1863, Pemberton called for the first council of war and asked his generals what to do. The generals decided Johnston should move north of Jackson, calling for Pemberton to move toward him. Pemberton told his men to march south then north and rendezvous with Johnston's force at Clinton. They were halfway there when the Federals intercepted them. On May 16, Grant fought the last battle of his field campaign, at Champion Hill, Mississippi. Pemberton had 23,000 men against McPherson's and McClernand's 32,000.

Pemberton deployed three divisions a mile east of Baker's Creek to cover the bridges on the Jackson and Raymond roads. His line extended four miles northeast to the crest of Champion Hill, then curved back two miles west to where the Jackson road crossed Baker's Creek. Major General Carter Stevenson commanded Pemberton's left, Major General John Bowen the center, and Major General William Loring the right.

The battle began in the south, where Major General Andrew Jackson Smith's Federal division, marching west on Raymond Road, came under fire from Loring's artillery. The heaviest fighting was to the north, where McClernand's XIII Corps was to strike the angle of Pemberton's line at Champion Hill from the east while Logan's division of McPherson corps attacked from the north. Only one of McClernand's divisions came into action and that was Brig. Gen. Alvin Hovey's. At 10:30 A.M., Hovey sent his two brigades to charge up Champion Hill. Holding the Confederate left was Gen. Stevenson. Some of his regiments were spread out over 300 yards. Before Stevenson was the Federal brigade of Brig. Gen. McGinnis. During the battle, Capt. Samuel Ridley's Mississippi Battery was captured and Ridley was hit six times.

By 1:00 P.M., the Confederate left was falling apart. At 1:30 P.M., Bowen began to move towards Pemberton. Bowen launched a counterattack against Hovey's troops with Col. Francis Cockrell's Missouri brigade on the left and Brig. Gen. Martin Green's Arkansas brigade on the right. Hovey retreated under the Confederate assault. Grant now ordered two brigades from the XVII Corps under Colonel's George Boomer and Samuel Holmes to help Hovey. On the right flank atop Champion Hill, the 34th Indiana was rallied by General Logan, who then led his men forward. General Peter Osterhaus forward. Hovey drove Pemberton's left back until the Confederate line faced almost due north. Union General Osterhaus advanced his men from the east and threatened Bowen's right flank. The Confederate defensive line at Champion Hill's collapsed and without any orders from General William Loring, his men decided to rush in and attack the fleeing Confederates.

Pemberton called a retreat and ordered Brig. Gen. Lloyd Tilghman to hold his opposition one mile east of the crossing. One of the last casualties was Tilghman himself, killed when solid shot from Federal cannon ripped through his hip. Pemberton made it across the Raymond Road Bridge; Loring's 6,550 men were cut off and he abandoned his artillery and supplies. Three days later he joined Johnston's army at Jackson. Union losses at Champion Hill were 2,441, and Pemberton lost 3,839. Pemberton took a beating there and pulled his army into the defense of Vicksburg.

Pemberton set up entrenchments along the Big Black River and sent Bowen and Brigadier General John Vaughn to protect the earthworks. On May 17, 1863, the Federals under Brigadier General Michael Lawler attacked the Confederates at Big Black River Bridge, fighting their way across the Big Black. The Confederates destroyed their river crossings behind them, but the Federals threw up their own bridges and continued the pursuit on the next day. Federal losses at Big Black Creek were 39 killed and 237 wounded, including Colonel William Kinsman of the 23rd Ohio. The Confederate losses were 200 men, killed, wounded or missing, with 1,751 being captured.

On May 18, 1863, approaching from the east and northeast, McClernand's, McPherson's, and Sherman's corps neared the Vicksburg defenses. Sherman veered north to take the hills overlooking the Yazoo River. Possession of these heights assured Grant reinforcement and supply lines from the North. On May 19, Grant made his first attack on the city's seven-mile long entrenchments. McClernand attacked on the east, and McPherson and Sherman on the north. Sherman's XV Corps made the initial assault. Colonel Stiles Smith, of the 1st Brigade, in Major General Frank Blair Jr.'s, 2nd Division, led his five regiments, the 113th, and the 116th Illinois, the 6th, and the 8th Missouri, and the 13th U.S., toward Stockade Redan. Captain Charles Ewing, of the 13th U.S. infantry, managed to gain only a foothold on a ditch north of the stockade but the stockade itself was not captured. Grant lost 942 men; Pemberton only lost 250. On May 22, 1863, the second assault was a disaster for Union forces. For four hours, the Federals attacked Railroad Redoubt and Colonel Ashbel Smith's 2nd Texas, just to the north.

The Federals were bogged down. Grant ordered another assault in mid-afternoon, based on McClernand's report that he had two forts on the Railroad Redoubt and that he needed Grant to send McPherson and Sherman to help him hold them. In actuality, McClernand had already lost his hold on the forts. Sherman and McPherson renewed their attacks based on McClernand's information. The Federals under their command took heavy losses, and could not break through the forts. The Federals lost 3,199 men and the Confederates lost 500 men. The attack showed the strength of the miles of Confederate works arching east around the city and convinced Grant that Pemberton could only be defeated in a protracted siege.

On May 22, 1863, the siege of Vicksburg began and lasted until July 4, 1863. As the siege progressed, Pemberton's 20,000-man garrison was reduced by disease and starvation and the city's residents were forced to seek the refuge of caves and bomb proofs in the surrounding hillsides where they sometimes ate rats to satisfy their great hunger. Grant was then being reinforced, and he soon had 70,000 men along a twelve-mile front. By mid-June, Grant had assembled 200 pieces of artillery. Grant tried several times to gain access to the fort by tunneling under it and trying to blow a hole to allow the infantry to charge into the city's earthworks.

On June 23, 1863, Captain Andrew Hickenlooper, Chief Engineer for the XVII Corps, dug a gallery forty-five feet long in two days, and the tunnel was filled with 2,200 pounds of black powder. The Confederates heard the digging, so they began to dig a counter tunnel but just before it was completed, the Federals exploded their tunnel, killing six Confederates. Brigadier General Mortimer Leggett's Federal brigade charged into the crater left by the explosion. But they did not bring ladders with them and could not get out to the front. The Confederates began firing right down on top of the Federals. At 5:00 P.M., the Yankees retreated from the crater and returned to their trenches. The Federals lost 200 men, and the Confederates also lost 200 men.

On July 1, 1863, Grant tried one more time to blow a hole under the same Confederate earthworks. Twelve Confederates were killed and 108 wounded in the blast. The Federals once again failed to take the earthworks. Grant opted for an all out assault on July 6, 1863, but on that same day, Johnston, who was in Jackson, was to attack Grant and help Pemberton. He had massed 30,000 men but he was too late. Hunger and daily bombardments by Grant's forces and Porter's gunboats compelled Pemberton to ask for surrender terms on July 3, 1863. Grant offered none and instead demanded unconditional surrender. Grant later changed his mind and decided to parole all of Pemberton's men if Pemberton would surrender the fort.

Pemberton surrendered the city on July 4, 1863, thus ending the Second Vicksburg Campaign. On July 4, 1863, thousands of Confederates were paroled so Sherman moved his force to oppose this new threat. Sherman's march would result in the siege of Jackson. On this same date, at a place called Gettysburg, Pennsylvania, Confederate General Robert E. Lee and the Army of Northern Virginia suffered a humiliating blow to their forces. On July 9, 1863, Port Hudson surrendered to the Federals. The Mississippi River was now open to Union shipping along its entire length.

Never Again

I met an interesting older gentleman at a Louisville bookstore. When I told him of my interest in ghost stories, he told me that he had an encounter with a restless spirit who long ago fought as a soldier in the Civil War.

This man grew up in Barren County, Kentucky. When he was young he sat before his grandfather and heard tales passed down about the Civil War and how it affected folks from that county. We'll call this man "Jim".

Years later Jim traveled to the Southeast to tour Civil War battle sites. He visited Vicksburg National Military Park via driving tour and by walking along the grassy paths. After reaching the top of a hill, he suddenly felt two invisible hands grab his shoulders and turn him around to face downhill.

Portrait of Pvt. William T. Carter (second from right in white collar) and group of 3rd Maryland Infantry.
Courtesy of the Library of Congress.

He heard a spectral voice insist, "This is what we saw that day!" Jim stared down the hillside trying to visualize the battle scene.

In his shock he waited a moment in silence and heard the spirit again speak, "Never again let this happen."

Jim felt that this message from a Civil War soldier, given on the very site of the bloody conflict, referred to the traumatic and senseless division, which split our dear country.

Dead Man's Walk

In addition to Jim's personal experience, he also heard this tale from his grandfather. A man from Barren County, who served for the Union cause, was taken prisoner and placed in the Confederate held prison at Andersonville, Georgia. Located in Sumter County, Georgia, and nicknamed

"Hell on Earth," Andersonville Prison or Camp Sumter opened in February of 1864, on 16.5 acres of open land, and was enclosed by a twenty-five foot tall wooden stockade fence. In June, the prison was expanded to twenty-six acres.

The prison, which was only designed to hold 10,000 men, eventually held 26,000 men. There was no medical care, no housing, and no clothing. Because of a drainage problem, fresh water became almost non-existent. Since the South was lacking food, the prisoners also suffered hunger. Scurvy, smallpox, and disease overran the camp. One Union soldier from Ohio noted that the prisoners were so thin from lack of food that it would take seven of them put together to "cast a shadow." Of the 45,000 men that would be held at Andersonville, 13,000 men would die.

There was a line that provided a clear stopping point for those who wished to stay inside and try to survive. Those with a strong desire to escape, who were suicidal or who had been driven insane, crossed outside the line. Confederate sentries in elevated "roosts" posted every thirty yards watched that line and instantly shot any who crossed and moved closer to the wooden fence. This line was known as the "Dead Line" and was nineteen feet before the fence. Reportedly, a soldier who killed someone who crossed Dead Line was rewarded with a month furlough to visit loved ones back home.

The Barren County soldier faced desperate circumstances and an unknown number of years as captive within the prison. All normal means of escape appeared to be cut off, and any attempt not only futile, but likely to end in instant execution. But this soldier thoughtfully watched the wagons and horse traffic, which moved in and out of the prison compound. One wagon that traveled outside every day was the death cart.

An army graveyard. Edwin Forbes, artist. *Courtesy of the Library of Congress.*

After putting himself on the detail for the removal of corpses from the camp to the wagon, he was able to spot a moment when the wagon was unwatched. He jumped inside and pulled several stiff bodies on top his own living one. Bearing the smell and weight of the corpses and fearing discovery at any moment, he nevertheless succeeded in his plan, traveling outside of the prison.

He managed to pull himself from the dead bodies en route to the graveyard and run to the woods. Now he was free to continue his escape, which meant a walk north across over half the state of Georgia and through Tennessee for nearly 500 miles into southern Kentucky. He traveled at night and kept to the countryside, trying to survive on berries, roots, and stolen food. Once he smelled corn bread cooling at a slave cabin's window and rushed up to grab it. The slaves just then returned from the fields and chased him into the kitchen.

He grabbed a kitchen knife, pointed it toward the African workers, and said, "I don't want to have to kill you for this food but I will!"

When the slaves discovered that he was "one of Lincoln's men," they welcomed him to all the food he needed for his journey.

Many times he slept in hay lofts. Confederate soldiers searched the back roads and farms for deserters or escaped Northern soldiers. One morning he awoke to hear the sound of bayonets thrust through the hay where he was concealed. One bayonet came within an inch of his wrist.

Incredibly, he made his journey all the way back to his beloved Kentucky. He walked to his own cabin door and knocked, expecting to embrace his wife. But, how haggard and thin and pale he looked, and indeed, when she went to look out the window, she thought him a ghost of her deceased spouse. She refused to let this ghost in the front door for three weeks!

Ghosts of Andersonville Prison

I contacted Kevin Frye of Butler, Georgia. Kevin is very knowledgeable about Andersonville and lives close to that historic site. He gave some background on escapes from Andersonville and noted an experience there.

Kevin Frye

There were 341 successful escapes from Andersonville. The majority included prisoners who were paroled outside the stockade for reasons of burial duty and other chores preformed for the guards. They most often overpowered the guards, bribed the guards, or slipped away when the guards were not looking.

Kevin Frye at the Andersonville's Prison graveyard, Georgia. *Courtesy Kevin Frye.*

I don't know of any spectacular events during any escapes. At least one man attempted an escape by having his fellow prisoner's tie his feet together, tie a rag around his jaw, and solemnly carry him to the dead house where the "dead man" waited for dark. As there was no need to guard the dead, he simply got up and ran. It's assumed several made it out this way before this method of escape was exposed. The graveyard is about half a mile to the north of the stockade and it is still an active national cemetery with an average of three burials of veterans each week.

I have had the pleasure of walking the stockade grounds alone at night, as well as the cemetery. I have never witnessed anything related to the supernatural; however, I have had unique experiences with my cameras.

Is a ghost in charge of my camera?

My daughter Ashley and I spent a night at the site of the Andersonville Civil War prison. Three other living historians and I participated in a weekend visit onsite. There was nothing advertised, just a spontaneous weekend. Anyway, we walked around the perimeter of the site at dusk and were at the place where the Raiders Gallows were and the execution took place just at dark.

We saw several deer run across the stockade. It was beautiful! There was another one to the west of the site where we were standing. I was talking to my wife on my cell phone, about nothing special, and a deer stood there about 100 yards away at the tree line where the "dead house" once stood. She watched us for every bit of ten minutes before slowly strolling off into the tree line. There is a large circle of eleven trees at that site.

I haven't been able to find the meaning behind why they were planted in that manner. This is where Ashley said she had this weird feeling that we should go take some photos. We proceeded by flashlight through the south gate, across the perimeter road, and into the field toward the circle of trees. We went into the circle.

Up to this point, I hadn't told Ashley this is where the dead house was located. My digital camera has an odd way of taking photos. You look through the viewer and there is a green light. You push the button down halfway and then the light flashes orange until it does an auto focus, which usually takes two seconds, and finally it turns green. You then push the button the rest of the way down and take the photo. We had just put in new batteries and taken several photos of Providence Spring and the gallows spot with no problem.

At the dead house location, Ashley attempted to take several photos. Nope, it was not going to take. The camera did its green, then flashing orange, but wouldn't go green or allow the photo to be taken. She and I tried to get it to work several times. There was nothing. I checked the battery meter and it was fully charged. All normal power showed to be good, but no photo. We continued around the rest of the stockade and past the hospital field. I tried again to take photos and it still wouldn't work.

We finished the rest of our walk going about half a mile. When we got back to the camper just for giggles, I tried the camera outside. It took a perfect photo. Go figure!

Grandfather's Spirit Led Me

Dorothy Kress

When I lived in Chicago I enjoyed going to the public library. I ended up doing some research there because my family told me that my great-great-grandfather from Tennessee ended up in Chicago at Camp Douglas. He was a Confederate prisoner and died there. My Mom's Great-Grandfather Lemuel Senn fought for the South. Nobody knew where he was buried, just that he died at Camp Douglas. I couldn't find records of this Camp Douglas anywhere!

I was so frustrated I spoke to his spirit, saying "Grandpa, if you want me to find you, help me!"

I walked down the aisle between the book stacks with my hand out and all of a sudden, this book was in my hand.

So I spoke again to his spirit, "Grandpa, if you're in this book, help me to find you."

I opened immediately to a paragraph about Camp Douglas. I actually found a photograph of the Camp Douglas Confederate Soldiers. I discovered there was a mass grave with a war memorial built on top of it. When I went there, I found it had his name on it, along with two other Senn's. I actually found three missing members of my family that day! I started asking around about Camp Douglas. Nobody at the library knew anything. I asked a college professor. He hadn't heard of it either.

But little by little, I began to pick up information about the history of Camp Douglas. It was open for only six months and in that short time six thousand Confederate prisoners died. They were there from winter into spring. I read that the prisoners made plans to break out and get guns and attack Union soldiers from the rear. I suspect that my Grandfather was one of those plotting to break out because he died along with his brother and cousin on the same day. His brother was named Samuel and his cousin was Daniel. My Grandfather had a large family with 12 kids. Maybe they were shot for planning the prison escape.

Union soldiers at Camp Douglass. *Courtesy of the Library of Congress.*

The Camp was located near 31st Street to 35th and Martin Luther King Drive. The Confederates were buried in a mass grave. During the cold weather, they were given one blanket for a cabin of men. The locals paid to see the prisoners. They held picnics outside the prison in view of the starving soldiers. The massive grave is at Oakwood Cemetery.

The Ghosts of Charit Creek

I spoke with a park ranger who has worked for twenty-two years at Charit Creek Lodge in the Big South Fork National River and Recreation Area. He noted that early settlers built the cabin in 1820, which later became Charit Creek Lodge. He said that one seasonal park ranger experienced something unusual years ago. The site was empty of visitors. While sleeping in one cabin, he awoke to see a ghostly figure standing on the opposite side of the cabin room.

He told other park staff that the man appeared in clothing typical of the 1800s. He said the man was tall, with a long beard. The description matched the look of a local man who was a century in the grave—William Riley Hatfield. Mr. Hatfield lived in the old homestead there and was killed by a neighbor. In a disagreement, the neighbor pulled a pistol and shot Hatfield. Mr. Hatfield is buried in a field next to Charit Creek Lodge. In recent years, Mr. Hatfield's descendants have traveled from Oklahoma, stayed in the Lodge, and presented the park staff with a photograph. In the photo, Mr. Hatfield has a long coat on and a gray beard.

The word, "Charit," is not in the English language, so what is likely is that Charit Creek is a shortened form of the name Charity. In that area, a nickname is often made by shortening someone's name. In this manner, Shadrick becomes Shay. There was a girl named Charity who, with her brother and parents, lived in this area in the 1920s. They were caught outside as a huge thunderstorm rained down, and as they tried to cross the creek to get home, Charity was carried away to the junction of Station Camp Creek and drowned. The park ranger spoke with an older woman who said she was born in the same house where Charity and her family once lived. She was born there shortly after the drowning. She claims that local folks and visitors have seen the ghost of Charity playing down at the creek.

Some of the earliest residents had the names of Blevins and Slaven. There seems to be no specific, written history on these families. However, a collection and partial transcription of oral tales from locals was done in the mid- to late 1970s. A book was written titled *History of No Business and Station Camp*. Charit Creek Lodge is located on Station Camp Creek. Jonathan Blevins settled at Station Camp Creek. He was a long rifle hunter. It is believed that he built the original cabin that became Charit Creek Lodge. He was buried two miles down Station Camp Creek. There is also a little cemetery 200 yards from the Lodge. Jonathan Burke was buried in that cemetery. There are only three headstones visible.

Two Boys Who Escaped the War but Lost Their Lives

There is also a small gravesite a half-mile upstream from the Charit Creek Lodge. It has two field stone grave markers of the two young Tackett boys who died. There is a faint scratching on the stone, which carries the date1863. In that year, Civil War guerrillas terrorized the pro-Union area residents, looking for young men to take prisoner. The mother of these two boys, knowing the boys would have no time to escape, put them under her feather mattress and lay on top of them, pretending to be sick. But the boys suffocated. It is sad that they were hidden to save their lives, but in the process they were accidentally killed. The little graveyard is protected by a rail fence, which was put in place by the Park Service. The old Tackett cabin site is still visible with only the chimney showing, and the graves are 150 feet behind the cabin site. People have reported glowing orbs or light near the graves of the boys.

The area was fairly lawless during the Civil War, with murders, thefts, and raids. It was not important strategically, so no armies were posted to uphold the rule of law. Folks outside the region, possibly from a few counties away, used the Civil War as an excuse to settle old grudges or simply to take advantage of the people. They stole horses, robbed, and killed.

One notorious guerilla with Southern sympathies was Champ Ferguson. He had a large group of 250 men, and some of his detachments could have been those who rode to the Tackett home. He called himself Captain, though he may not have been so authorized. He was from Clinton County, Kentucky. He later settled near Sparta, Tennessee. He was one of only two men of rank executed for war crimes, in addition to the commander of Andersonville Prison. He was tried, convicted, and executed in 1865 at a military prison in Nashville.

The locals formed a Home Guard and fought a small skirmish, killing some of the guerrillas in the summer of 1863. That was called either the Battle of Duck Shoals or Battle of Big Branch Creek. Many old homesteads were abandoned in the 1940s and 1950s and have since disappeared.

Ghost Soldiers Joined the Re-Enactment

Three Tales by Terrell Bryant

Back in the early 1990s we were down at Grayson Springs, in Grayson County, Kentucky. They don't do that re-enactment any more. It was raining that night and early the next morning. We formed up for battle for the Union.

Re-enactor Terrell Bryant at the Old Bardstown Village, Kentucky. *Photo by Thomas Freese.*

A guy came up and told us that there were trenches cut up in the bottom of the hill. He told us they were going to be in the first trench only as they didn't have enough re-enactors to fill the other trenches behind that one. So they told us to take it easy and not overrun the first trench since there weren't enough re-enactors to cover the other two trenches.

We formed up and started marching over to where the battlefield was—this was the actual battlefield of Grayson Springs. Right as we arrived at the battlefield the rain quit, the sun came out, and shone just as pretty as you could ever see right on this hillside. Me and my other re-enactors looked up and saw silvery metal—like off hundreds of gun barrels—glittering all over the side of the hill.

We laughed and said, "Man, they lied to us! There are plenty of them all over the hill in all three trenches!"

We took off to start the attack then fell back and resumed the attack. On our third advance we overran the other re-enactors in the first trench.

They looked at us, astounded, and said, "What are you all doing? There's nobody else up there."

We insisted, "Oh yeah there is! We saw the sun shining off all your gun barrels. We know there's more up there. You just don't want to tell us!"

They repeated, "No, we're telling you, there's nobody else up there."

After the battle was over, we went up on the hill past the first trench. When we got to the second trench, we clearly saw no re-enactors and there was not a single footprint in the mud.

Union Soldier Wandered into the Rebel Camp

On another re-enactment in Kentucky, we camped out and sat around talking until late in the night. We clustered around the fire near our tent on this Saturday night. We were dressed as Confederates for that battle. A Union soldier walked up to our fire and stood near us.

One of our men asked him, "Do you want a drink?"

The man said, "Yeah, sure."

The Union soldier reached out for the drink. But when one of our men, dressed in gray, reached out to hand him the cup, the Union soldier glanced down and saw the color of his jacket in the firelight. He spun around to start running but simply disappeared in midair. This happened right in front of all of us.

It was the weirdest thing I've ever seen in my life.

Ghost Soldier Helps Himself to an Apple

One time we camped out for a re-enactment down in Cadiz, Kentucky. We were dressed as Confederates. One of our guys brought some apples to share.

He said, "Guys, I got some apples for you all. They're on a bowl sitting on the table. If you want some apples, help yourself.

"That's just something extra we had left over from making a pie."

A guy in a Confederate uniform came walking up to our camp. He was dressed as a private. He looked just like any of the re-enactors. The etiquette in re-enactments is to not walk through somebody else's camp

Confederate camps located on Starkweather's Hill, Perryville, Kentucky.

unless you know someone in the camp. Or at least you talk to them, politely introducing yourself. That's common courtesy.

So the Confederate man walked past everyone and right over to pick up one of the apples. Everyone was trying to figure out who he was. Then he just walked away.

I said, "Man did you see that? Can you believe that guy? He walked over and took one of your apples!"

Our friend agreed, "I can't believe he just walked right up and took one of my apples!"

We walked to the table and I asked, "How many apples did you bring?"

He said, "Well I thought I brought six apples."

I looked and saw there were still six apples on the table.

I added, "Man, you must have brought seven because there are still six here."

He countered, "I guess I must have miscounted…"

We sat back down and later that same evening the **same guy** walked up to the table.

I thought *this guy has some nerve to come walking back to our camp after he stole an apple from us.*

He didn't say a word as everybody sat and watch him walk right over to the table. Everyone saw him pick up an apple. Then he walked off.

I got up and went over to the table. There were still six apples on the table. I don't know if he was a ghost or a good magician, but everyone saw him take an apple.

Four re-enactors at Old Bardstown Village. Pictured from left to right are Sgt. Warren Pike, Cpl. Gene Autry Allen, 1ST Sgt. Jim Dunn, and Pvt. Josh Lewis. *Photo by Thomas Freese.*

Endnotes

1. Thomas Livermore, *Numbers and Losses In the Civil War in America: 1861-1865* (Carlisle, Pa: John Kallmann Publishers, 1900, reprint, 1996), 1-9.
2. Stephen Foster. *Statistics of War* (Atlas Edition).
3. Thomas Clark, *Kentucky: Land of Contrast* (New York: Harper & Row Publishers, 1968), 143.
4. Bryan Bush, *The Civil War Battles of the Western Theater* (Paducah: Turner Publishing, 1998, reprint, 2000), 180.
5. Bush, *The Civil War Battles of the Western Theater*, 181.
6. Ibid., 181.
7. Ibid., 181-182.
8. Ibid., 182.
9. Mary E. Stucky, July 1863, Diary (Jeffersontown, Kentucky: Union Literary Institute).

Battle of Perryville
1. Bryan Bush, The Civil War Battles of the Western Theater, (Paducah: Turner Publishing, 1998, reprint 2000), 36.
2. Ibid., 37.
3. Ibid., 37.
4. Ibid., 38.
5. Ibid., 39.
6. Ibid., 40.
7. Ibid., 40.
8. Ibid., 40.
9. Ibid., 41.
10. Ibid., 41.
11. Ibid., 41.
12. Ibid., 41.
13. Sam Watkins, Co. "Aytch" First Tennessee Regiment or a Side Show of the Big Show, edited by Ruth Hill Fulton McAllister, (Franklin, Tennessee: Providence House Publishers, 2007), 61.
14. Dr. J. J. Polk, Autobiography of Dr. J. J. Polk, (Louisville, Kentucky: J. Morton & Company, 1867), 97.
15. Kenneth Hafendorfer, Perryville: Battle for Kentucky, (Louisville, Kentucky: K. H. Press, 1991), 422-423.

Camp Boone
1. William Davis, *The Orphan Brigade: The Kentucky Confederates Who Couldn't Go Home* (Doubleday & Co., Inc., 1980), 13-24.
1a. Davis, William, The Orphan Brigade: The Kentucky Confederates Who Couldn't Go Home, (Doubleday & Co., Inc., 1980)

Battle of Franklin, Tennessee
1. Bryan Bush, *The Civil War Battles of the Western Theater* (Paducah: Turner Publishing, 1998, reprint 2000), 87.
2. Ibid., 87.
3. Ibid., 88.
4. Ibid., 88.

5. Ibid., 89.
6. Ibid.
7. Ibid., 89.
8. Ibid.

Battle of Stone's River, Tennessee

1. Bryan Bush, *The Civil War Battles of the Western Theater* (Paducah, Kentucky: Turner Publishing, 1998, reprint, 2000), 49.
2. Bush, 49.
3. Ibid., 50.
4. Ibid., 50.
5. Ibid., 50.

Battle of Bardstown, Kentucky

1. Bryan Bush, *Terry's Texas Rangers: The 8th Texas Cavalry* (Paducah, Kentucky: Turner Publishing, Inc., 2002), 41.
2. Ibid., 48.

Fort Duffield, Kentucky

1. Richard Briggs, *West Point and the Civil War* (West Point, Kentucky: Top's Books, 1993), 8.
2. Ibid., 10.
3. Ibid., 18.

Camp Nelson, Kentucky

1. Stephen McBride, *Camp Nelson: A Fortified Union Supply Depot, Recruitment Center, and African American Refugee Camp, Kentucky's Civil War 1860-1865*, 2002-2003 Edition (Back Home in Kentucky), 38-39.
2. Camp Nelson Restoration and Preservation Foundation.

The Battle of Sacramento, Kentucky

1. Thomas Jordan & J. P. General Pryor, *The Campaigns of General Nathan Bedford Forrest and of Forrest's Cavalry*, (New Orleans, 1868, New York: Da Capo Press, 1996).
2. Southern Historical Society Papers. *His First Battle, Forrest and his Campaigns*, 456-457.
3. "Forrest's Old Regiment." *Confederate Veteran*, 40-41
4. John Wyeth. "Appearance and Characteristics of Forrest." *Confederate Veteran.*
5. Official Records of the War of the Rebellion:
a. O.R. Series I-Vol. 7, December 28, 1861-Action at Sacramento, Ky. No. 1 reports of Brig. Gen. Thomas Crittenden, U.S. Army.
b. O.R. Series I-Vol. 7 December 28, 1861-Action at Sacramento, Ky.-No. 3 Report of Col. Nathan Bedford Forrest, Forrest's regiment, C. S. Army.
c. O.R. Series I-Vol. 7-December 28, 1861-Action at Sacramento, Ky. No. 2 Report of Brig. Gen. Charles Clark, C. S. Army.

The Battle of Fort Pillow, Tennessee

1. Patricia Faust, editor, *Historical Times Illustrated Encyclopedia of the Civil War* (New York: Harper Collins Publishers, 1986), 277.
2. Stephen Foster, *Battle of Fort Pillow* Atlas Editions.

Bibliography

Books

Briggs, Richard. *West Point and the Civil War*. West Point, Kentucky: Top's Books, 1993.

Bush, Bryan. *The Civil War Battles of the Western Theater*.Paducah: Turner Publishing, Inc. 1998, reprint 2000.

Bush, Bryan. *Terry's Texas Rangers: The 8th Texas Cavalry*.Paducah: Turner Publishing, Inc., 2002.

Clark, Thomas. *Kentucky: Land of Contrast*. New York: Harper & Row Publishers, 1968.

Davis, William. *The Orphan Brigade: The Kentucky Confederates Who Couldn't Go Home*. Doubleday & Co., Inc., 1980.

Faust, Patricia, editor. *Historical Times Illustrated Encyclopedia of the Civil War*. Harper Collins Publishers, 1986.

Foster, Stephen. *Battle of Fort Pillow*. Atlas Editions, 1993.

Hafendorfer, Kenneth. *Perryville: Battle for Kentucky*.Louisville, Kentucky: K. H. Press, 1991.

Jordan, Thomas & J. P. General Pryor. *The Campaigns of General Nathan Bedford Forrest and of Forrest's Cavalry, New Orleans, 1868*. New York, New York: Da Capo Press, 1996.

Livermore, Thomas. *Numbers and Losses In the Civil War in America: 1861-1865*. Carlisle, Pennsylvania: John Kallmann Publishers, 1900, reprint, 1996.

McBride, Stephen. "Camp Nelson: A Fortified Union Supply Depot, Recruitment Center, and African American Refugee Camp," *Kentucky's Civil War 1860-1865*. Clay City, Kentucky, Back Home in Kentucky, Inc. 2005.

Polk, J. J. *Autobiography of Dr. J. J. Polk*. Louisville, Kentucky: J. Morton & Company, 1867.

Stuckey, Mary. *July 1863, Diary of*. Unpublished, Union Library Institute, Jeffersontown, Kentucky.

The War of the Rebellion: A Compilation of the Official Records of the Union and Confederate Armies. 128 vols., Washington, D. C.: Government Printing Office, 1880-1901.

Watkins, Sam. *Co. "Aytch" First Tennessee Regiment or a Side Show of the Big Show*. Edited by Ruth Hill Fulton McAllister. Franklin, Tennessee: Providence House Publishers, 2007.

Magazines

Confederate Veteran
Southern Historical Society Papers

Other Books by the Authors

Books by Bryan Bush

"Butcher Burbridge:" Union General Stephen Gano Burbridge and His Reign of Terror Over Kentucky. Morely, Missouri: Acclaim Press, Inc., 2008.

The Civil War Battles of the Western Theater. Paducah, Kentucky: Turner Publishing, 1998, reprint 2000.

Kentucky's Civil War: 1861-1865. Clay City, Kentucky: Back Home in Kentucky, Inc., 2005.

Lincoln and the Speeds: The Untold Story of a Devoted and Enduring Friendship. Morley, Missouri: Acclaim Press, 2008.

Lloyd Tilghman: Confederate General in the Western Theater. Morley, Missouri: Acclaim Press, 2007.

Louisville and the Civil War: A History and Guide. Charleston, South Carolina: The History Press, 2009.

www.BryanSBush.com

Books by Thomas L. Freese

Fog Swirler and 11 Other Ghost Stories. Bloomington, Indiana: Author House, 2006.

Ghosts, Spirits, and Angels: True Tales from Kentucky and Beyond. Morley, Missouri: Acclaim Press, 2009.

How to Make Southwest Jewelry in Wood. Atglen, Pennsylvania: Schiffer Publishing, 2010.

Shaker Ghost Stories from Pleasant Hill, Kentucky. Bloomington, Indiana: Author House, 2005.

Strange and Wonderful Things: a Collection of Ghost Stories with Special Appearances by Witches and Other Bizarre Creatures. Frederick, Maryland: Publish America, 2008.

www.ThomasL.Freese.com

Hcatd − 6/12/19−BT